FOREWORD

THIS BIOGRAPHY OF William Carey has been prepared
for the bicentenary of his birth, which falls on 17th
August 1961. Since all previous lives are now out
of print, it was necessary for a new study to be prepared. As I am the present General Home Secretary of
the Society that Carey formed and have had the advantage of at least a brief visit to India and particularly to
Serampore, it is fitting perhaps that I should attempt the
task. My debts to earlier biographers, particularly to
George Smith and S. Pearce Carey, and also to Dr. E. A.
Payne for his various writings on the people and the
period, are obvious and I cordially acknowledge them.
I am grateful also to Miss Kathleen P. Hawkins for her
excellent help in typing the manuscript. The more I
have studied Carey the greater my admiration for the
man and his work, and I trust that this life of him will
in some small degree set free for the help and benefit of
another generation his contribution to the world missionary movement and to the Church of God every-
where.

J. B. M.

TO MY WIFE

CONTENTS

Carey and his pundit.

FRONTISPIECE

ON THE 11th November 1793, the Danish sailing ship the *Krön Princessa Maria* dropped anchor in Calcutta after a tedious and at times dangerous five months' voyage from Copenhagen to Serampore. The ship's company was small and the passengers few; but on that day history was made. The name of the sturdy and stocky Englishman who stepped ashore, never to return to his native land, was William Carey. Obscure and unknown at the time, now, more than a century-and-a-half later, he has a name of growing world significance. The late William Paton once declared to the present writer that the missionary movement had not yet caught up with William Carey. He was not an explorer or a trader; not a soldier or an administrator; nor was he an adventurer or a ne'er do well; he represented a movement that would in time reveal itself as the redeeming feature of England's relationships with the East and Africa. Too much must not be claimed for William Carey, however, in the history of Missions. As will be seen later, he had predecessors. He was neither the "Father of Modern Missions" nor their "Pioneer"; other Englishmen had gone out as missionaries to the heathen and other missionaries had gone to India from other places. His title to fame, and it is notable, is that he founded the Baptist Missionary Society, and in so doing, as Dr. Latourette has said, "began a new era in Protestant Missions not only in India but in the entire world." "He represented a distinct point of departure in the history of Christianity," another historian has said. He was the first missionary of the Christian Gospel sent overseas by a small denominational group, expressly organized for such a purpose, and he and his colleague, John Thomas, were the first of their kind. In him, the original mission of the Church, as commanded by our Lord and as set out dramatically in the Acts of the Apostles, was rediscovered in prayer, thought and action. In him the churches of the eighteenth century launched themselves on a positive attacking policy that still goes on unfalteringly. Through him, the great international and interdenominational missionary movement that has marked the nineteenth and twentieth centuries came into action both in his own country and on a foreign shore. This Baptist pastor from Leicester, thirty-two years of age, who for much of his working life had been a shoemaker, became the prophet and apostle of an enterprise whose goal was the winning of the whole human race for Jesus Christ.

Of the voyage in the Danish East Indiaman, Carey wrote in his Journal, "For nearly a month we have been within two hundred miles of Bengal but the violence of the currents set us back when we have been at the very door. I hope I have learned the necessity of bearing up in the things of God against wind and tide." This ship was not their first choice. Carey and his colleague, Dr. John Thomas, were denied a passage in the *Earl of Oxford*—Thomas's debts having caught up with him—and, as a consequence, their waiting to board this ship at Ryde in the Isle of Wight was in vain. The *Earl of Oxford* being an English ship, there would have been difficulties in disembarking in the East India Company's India.

This trading company, overtaken as it was by political and administrative responsibility and afraid of elements that might disturb, had gone back on an earlier policy that looked favourably at missionary activity. In this same year, 1793, in a hysterical declaration, they had denounced missions as "indefensible" and as "striking against reason and sound policy." Indeed, by an earlier regulation, no English subject could land or reside in their domain except as licensed, and licences were not available to missionaries. In the case of passengers in a Danish vessel, however, these difficulties did not arise. By the time the *Krön Princessa Maria* was ready to sail from Dover on the 13th June, John Thomas had been able to overcome Mrs. Carey's tearful and oft-repeated refusals to accompany the party. Consequently, when Carey arrived in India, his wife, his wife's sister and his children, including a baby of six months or so, were with him. He had been prepared to make the voyage with one son only, Felix, returning for his wife and the other children later, but the family were now together in this venture. In a farewell letter to his bewildered father, who thought him mad, he described what he desired to do as "the most arduous, honourable and important work" that anyone could be called on to engage in.

This arrival in India in middle life was therefore a culmination of earlier thoughts and actions as well as an entry upon a new life in a sub-continent. The following chapters trace, first of all, Carey's early life in Northamptonshire and neighbourhood, and later seek to describe the way he fulfilled his call in far-off India.

Part I

LIFE IN ENGLAND

I. *The Boy Grows Up*

CAREY WAS BORN on 17th August 1761, at Paulerspury, a pleasant little village in Northamptonshire. Paulerspury was in the heart of agricultural England and nowhere near the sea. He was the eldest of the five children of a weaver, who later turned schoolmaster. They were miserably poor and seemingly without prospects. How likely it was that his village would remain the tiny stage on which the whole of his life would be lived. An uncle of his, however, had broken through the circle; he had emigrated to Canada and then returned, full of stories of other lands. But the family stock was good, though his youngest sister, Mary (Polly), after growing up, was for years a bed-ridden cripple, though a lively correspondent.

In Carey's early boyhood, signs began to accumulate that, as the Scots say, he was a "lad of pairts." Increasingly, the neighbours began to take note of him. There was a determination about him. When he fell from a tree, his first self-appointed task after recovery was to reach the top in triumph. Later in life he said of himself, "I can plod. I can persevere in any definite pursuit. To this I owe everything." In the whole of his story, whether in the formation of the B.M.S., the mastery of languages, the founding of Serampore College, or the development of the Mission, his well-knit compact figure could be seen steadily pacing out its appointed way. It was the same plodding and determined step that took him from Paulerspury, with its grass expanses and its fine estates, its production of iron and its manufacture of shoes, to a far-off shore.

In the family cottage, William Carey was fortunate enough to have a tiny room of his own and Polly, often his companion in his walks, describes it as having insects stuck in every corner and with live birds of all kinds. She declared him to be as earnest in his recreations as he was in school. Plodding along the country roads, he took time to observe carefully all he saw. He was a collector with natural history as his inspiration and the creator of the Serampore garden can be traced in this village lad and his scientific enthusiasm for nature. But this room of his was also a library, though most of its contents were borrowed. It was said of him that he starved himself to "buy the books he felt he needed." He was fully bent on reading all he could, though he was never a bookworm. His diary at a much later date tells how that at this time, when he was about fourteen, he chose to read books of science, history, voyages, etc., rather than any others. Novels and books of religion disgusted him. It was a little earlier, however, at the age of twelve that he first embarked on that study of languages which was to make him a literary phenomenon. It was Latin on which he first practised this genius of his, the book being Dyche's *Latin Vocabulary* and, by way of thoroughness, he learned most of its contents off by heart. Then later he was given a Latin grammar. By this time, also, Greek had captured his interest through a few characters he happened to drop on in a commentary. In this, he had the help of a dissipated youth, Thomas Jones, whose bad habits had brought him from college to weaving in the locality. His Hebrew he learned from neighbouring ministers with the help of books that were theirs. Dutch he picked up from a book found in an old woman's cottage. French he learned so as to write it in three weeks from a book purchased for a few coppers. Here, then, was an obvious growing point, and there must have been those in the neighbourhood who began to picture a future for him, perhaps away from his birth-place.

But up to the age of twenty-eight, William Carey was a shoemaker by trade and livelihood. Possibly he would have been a labourer all his life had not his father, realizing his unfitness for work in the fields owing to a painful skin disease, apprenticed him to the trade in boots and shoes. How often Carey could be seen tramping the roads of Northamptonshire with his burden of finished work on his back. His employer was the rough-tongued and hot-tempered Clarke Nichols of Hackleton, nine miles from Paulerspury. It was in the setting of this "cottage-workshop" that Carey found the Gospel that was to be both the inspiration of his life and the message that he was to take overseas.

II. The Making of a Pastor and Preacher

CAREY WAS BORN into a Church of England home. His grandfather and his father were both parish clerks at the Paulerspury Church where the Baptist Missionary Society placed a commemorative tablet to William Carey on 19th April 1944. His parents were Anglicans of good standing, though the Anglicanism of the time was disfigured by pluralities and other scandals. He himself as a youth had a declared and cordial hatred of Dissenters and we are told would not have been unwilling to see their meeting houses destroyed! But it turned out that his fellow-apprentice in Clarke Nichols' workshop, John Warr, was actually a member of one of these detested sects. In quite a short time, thanks to the daily importunity of this vigorous young disciple, Carey was attempting to control his language, attending the Anglican Church three times each Sunday, saying his prayers privately and visiting the Dissenters' prayer meetings. When he paid his monthly visit to Paulerspury, he requested that he might conduct family prayers, and this request was granted him. In this speedy reformation there was something of the pharisee, but the phase in this form was temporary. That his spiritual pilgrimage was of something of the order of Augustine and John Bunyan can be seen from the way in which he suffered in conscience and in mind after using a counterfeit shilling given to him as a Christmas box by a customer to defraud his employer, Clarke Nichols. On 10th February 1779, at the age of seventeen, there came the break with the Church of England, a breach that distressed his family greatly. The occasion was a sermon by a Congregationalist in the Hackleton meeting house on the text, "Let us go forth therefore unto him without the camp, bearing his reproach" (Hebrews xiii. 13). Interpreting this as a call to leave his family church and to associate with the Dissenters, Carey says that after this time he always attended Divine Worship with them. His identification with the Baptists, however, did not come until 5th October 1783, when at the age of twenty-two he was baptized in the River Nen by the Rev. John Ryland, junior. Carey had come across a newly published little book with a typical eighteenth century title, *Help to Zion's Travellers; being an attempt to remove various Stumbling Blocks out of the way, relating to Doctrinal Experimental and Practical Religion.* Its author, Robert Hall, the father of the outstanding Baptist preacher of the day, was himself the Baptist pastor at Arnsby, Leicestershire. The care with which Carey read and mastered this little volume with "its attempt to relieve discouraged Christians" can be seen in the summaries of its arguments written in his own neat hand in the copy which can now be found in Bristol Baptist College. Of it he said, "I do not remember to have read any book with such raptures." Carey remained a convinced Baptist to the end of his days, although his circle of acquaintances and friends both in England and India included many members of other denominations, many of them people of culture and influence. But there seems to be no evidence available from his letters as to why among the Dissenters he chose the Baptists. All that he wrote about the subject at the time was in the following laconic words, "I do not recollect having read anything on the subject before I applied to Mr. Ryland, senior, to baptize me. He lent me a pamphlet and turned me over to his son." Later, in 1814, writing to his son Jabez about missionary service in Amboyna, Carey bade him prove from Scripture to his hearers, "What is the right mode of baptism and who are the proper persons to be baptized?"

Carey had done a little preaching, rather unwillingly, before he was baptized. Already, as a small boy, his companions had often chaffed him, "Well, if you won't play, preach us a sermon." Clambering up on an old wyche elm some seven feet high, he had done as they asked. Then later came the time when his father succeeded in hearing him at a service without himself being seen. One of his daughters wrote, "We are convinced he approved what he heard and was highly gratified by it." About this time, à certain gentleman said, "Never a youth promised fairer to make a great man if he had not turned cushion thumper." An old woman with more spiritual discernment declared that he would be a great preacher, she thought, if he were spared. Then it was arranged that he should preach regularly to a small company at Earl's Barton, and this he did for three years or more with no financial profit to himself, trudging with plodding steps the six miles from Hackleton and back. The little house at Hackleton has been called "Carey's College," for, in common with many another cobbler's workshop, it was a meeting place for would-be scholars and ready debaters. The rough-hewn sign-board "Second-hand shoes and boots . . ." (now at Regent's Park College, Oxford), hardly suggested a place of learning, but at least, so someone said, one of the apprentices (a sensible-looking lad) always had a book

Carey's cottage at Moulton.

Serampore College.

at hand and listened with "intelligence and feeling to the better type of conversation." Here also Carey began to be marked out as "a very consistent and promising character." On the death of Clarke Nichols, his first employer, he transferred his apprenticeship to a Mr. T. Old, also of Hackleton. Then, when this second employer died, he took over his employer's liabilities and also married, on 10th June 1781, the widow's sister, Dorothy Plackett, five years his senior, a marriage increasingly shadowed over twenty-six years by her mental deterioration. Here was a cross whose nature would have broken many lesser men. Later he moved the shop to Piddington, where ague and fever resulted in life-long baldness, but he continued his preaching.

A series of church meeting minutes recorded at Olney, covering the period 17th June 1785 to 29th April 1787, shows Carey applying to the church at Olney, whose minister was John Sutcliff, to admit him to membership and to send him out into the work of the Ministry. There is a curious entry in the Hackleton Church records to the effect that he "whent away without his dismission." Nevertheless he was evidently concerned that everything should be done in order at Olney, and he submitted himself for interview and a period of trial preaching, culminating in his being "sent out by the church to preach the Gospel, *wherever God in his providence might call him*" (author's italics); a phrase with a prophetic ring as if already there was the sound of ocean breakers and a call to service far away. But his immediate destination was Moulton, a few miles from Hackleton. Here he remained until 1789, when he became the pastor of Harvey Lane, Leicester, a ministry he fulfilled until his departure to India in 1793.

B

III. The Missionary "Enthusiast"

IT WAS AT MOULTON that Carey's missionary passion finally declared itself. The sphere was difficult; the church, though small, was far from united. Happily, in a short time, the church had to be enlarged and a better spirit prevailed. After a period as their regular preacher (his pulpit can still be seen), he was ordained as pastor on 10th August 1786, by Ryland, Sutcliff and Fuller (all future associates in his great enterprise). The stipend was a mere pittance and, though Carey was again a shoemaker, after a spell of day-school teaching made impossible by his inability to maintain discipline, he and his growing family (despite a loss by bereavement) were desperately poor. But in the little cottage at Moulton, still to be seen with its commemorative tablet and the little sink where Carey soaked his leather, the Church of Jesus Christ rediscovered her primary task and received again the call to obey Christ's never-abrogated command, "Go ye therefore into all the world . . ." Visitors calling on the Carey family could not fail to notice on the wall "a very large map consisting of several sheets of paper pasted together by himself, on which he had drawn, with a pen, a place for every nation in the known world." Also, in his geography lessons at school, he used a globe he had made himself. Here was the visible sign of his concern for the whole world. He was collecting facts about the peoples of every race, tongue and religion, a pursuit he later com-

18

mended to his son Jabez on taking up residence in Amboyna. From that cobbler's bench in a tiny cottage in an obscure village in rural England, he sketched, in a scientific hand, the pattern of the world of his day. His famous little book with its typically lengthy eighteenth-century title, *An Enquiry into the Obligations of Christians to use Means for the Conversion of the Heathens, in which the Religious State of the Different Nations of the world, the Success of Former Undertakings and the Practicability of Further Undertakings, are considered*, by William Carey, was the published result of these researches. The problem of publishing was solved by a Baptist layman who gave him £10 for the purpose. This *Enquiry*, issued in 1792, when he had moved to Leicester, was perhaps the first "blue book" ever compiled, and even now, over a century-and-a-half later, it is only the statistical pages that are out of date. He surveyed the world in its customary divisions, Europe, Asia, Africa and America, taking notice of "the extent of the several countries, their population, civilization and religion." Here for all time, with an absence of rhetoric, is the classical presentation of the argument for the World Mission of the Church.

The handling of scripture was firm, and the great commission which had never yet been fulfilled was declared to be as binding on the Church in all succeeding generations as it was on the first disciples. Just as traders receiving a charter pressed it to its utmost limits, seeking its circumference, so the Church, charged by her Lord with the winning of the world, would do well to follow their courageous and persevering example. Earlier attempts at evangelizing other lands by the Church in different centuries were fairly described and assessed with glowing tributes to their brave pioneers.

He referred especially to the Moravians and to Eliot and Brainerd, the Brainerd who cried "O that I were a flaming fire in the service of my God." Practical difficulties were then faced and disposed of in terms of eighteenth-century opportunities. "Distances," thanks to the mariner's compass, could now be overcome; "Barbarism" was faced by traders as it was by the original apostles, why not then by missionaries? He confidently declared that in the course of time these barbarians, converted and civilized, would be preaching and writing to the glory of the Redeemer's name; "Death" might result, but did not Paul and Barnabas hazard their lives?; Absence of the "Necessaries" of life could soon be inventively overcome; Lastly, and how triumphantly in his own person and work he disposed for ever of this objection, "the Unintelligibility of their languages." His brief but excellent publication, sold, by the way, for 1s. 6d., concluded with a practical proposal that a Society, if possible of all denominations, or failing that of particular Baptists, be formed. Perhaps the most remarkable fact about the *Enquiry* was the way in which it was fulfilled, almost in detail.

But none of the churches of his day, Baptist or other, was ready as yet to follow his lead, although some of the ministers nearest to Carey, and what a fine group of young men they were, were on the brink of favourable decision. They had already been helped to this end years before, in 1784, when a "Call to Prayer" was issued at Nottingham at Sutcliff's suggestion, and in Ryland's drafting, pressing for a monthly prayer meeting on the first Monday of every month. This was no sectarian impulse, for Ryland wrote not simply as a Baptist minister but "in the whole interest of the Redeemer." Indeed, the primary impulse for this movement of intercession may be said to have been the American theologian Jonathan Edwards in his *Humble Attempt to Promote Explicit Agreement and Visible Union of God's People in Extraordinary Prayer for the Revival of Religion and the Advancement of Christ's Kingdom on Earth.*

In his *Enquiry*, Carey, recognizing the power of prayer, particularly in reference to the years since 1784, was at pains to point out that to be contented with prayer without exerting ourselves in the use of "means" was altogether reprehensible. Carey had been rebuked by an aged minister at Northampton in 1786 as "a miserable enthusiast" and told to sit down for asking for a ministerial discussion of the obligatory character of Christ's great commission to all disciples of all ages. His conversations and pleadings were now, in 1792, about to reap their harvest, not in the wedding of his Christian fellow-countrymen and the whole of his denomination to his conclusions, but a sufficient few! On 31st May this same year, the year also of the publishing of the *Enquiry*, Carey was the chosen preacher at the meetings of the Northamptonshire Baptist Association at Nottingham. His sermon on this occasion has been called the "Deathless Sermon." Its text was Isaiah 54. 2-3, and its powerful argument was summed up in the tremendous couplet:

> "Expect great things from God,
> Attempt great things for God."

But the service ended, the worshippers were dispersing and there was no sign of action when Carey took what proved to be a decisive step. He seized the arm of a fellow-minister and asked, almost in despair, "And are you after all again going to do nothing?" The man he

thus addressed was Andrew Fuller. Carey's instinct was
unerring, for here was possibly the only man in the
group whose courage and faith could match this thing.
Fuller had been born and brought up in the Fen country
and, after being called by his fellow-members to the
pastorate of the church at Soham, moved to Kettering,
where he ministered from 1783 to 1815. Like Carey, he
was a figure of controversy, but not so much in the
practical sphere of Christian duty as in the intellectual
realm of Christian theology. In 1784 he had published
a work entitled *Gospel Worthy of All Acceptation, or
the duty of Sinners to believe in Christ.* Its purpose
was to break the charmed circle of Baptist Calvinism
and to persuade his fellow-ministers and church members to believe that it was their duty to offer salvation
to all. He argued that there was "a general atonement
sufficient for the sins of the race and not a particular
atonement for the elect only" (Vedder, *History of the
Baptists*). Without this explosive material in the field
of doctrine, it is doubtful whether Carey could ever
have succeeded in his practical appeal. Fuller's use of
the word "Duty" was matched by his own word in the
Enquiry: "Obligation." Men whose gospel was only for
the few, a privileged minority, would hardly bestir
themselves to send out the good news to all men every-
where. But if the Gospel were for all, then all who had
been entrusted with it must carry it to all the world.
Fuller also, beginning to share Carey's impatience at all
the procrastination, had actually preached on the "Sin
of Delay," but now the moment had come. He gave
William Carey, in Nottingham, the answer he was waiting for, and in four short months, on 2nd October 1792,
at Kettering, in Widow Wallis's parlour, the Baptist
Missionary Society was formed.

IV. Forming a Missionary Society

VOLUNTARY SOCIETIES FOR this or that religious or social, scientific or philanthropic purpose were one of the happiest habits of the eighteenth century, and, whatever the casualties among them, the society Carey was so instrumental in forming has lasted till now. The very house in which it was brought into being, called the "Gospel Inn" because of the ready hospitality given by Widow Wallis, still stands in Lower Street, Kettering, and the right of access to the historic back parlour is in the terms of the present lease.

The Nottingham meeting of the Association had ended with a proposition moved by Andrew Fuller to the effect that "A plan be prepared against the next ministers' meeting at Kettering for forming a Baptist Society for propagating the Gospel among the Heathens." The consequence of this was that on 2nd October, after "the public services of the day, the ministers withdrew for further consultation," for the final battle, as it turned out, before Carey won his victory. One wonders how and by whom the argument was sustained in this little group of fourteen men, nearly all under forty, and who was the last to be won over. The result, however, was decisive action, despite the youthfulness of the group, their comparative poverty and the reluctance of the greater part of the denomination. A unanimous resolution was passed, arrived at without much delay, to the effect that a Society be formed with the title "The Particular Baptist Society for Propagating the Gospel among the Heathen."

In this resolution Carey's *Enquiry* was significantly referred to and the pattern outlined therein largely followed. The present divided state of Christendom was declared to make impossible anything but a denomination "exerting itself separately." A subscription list was opened and there were twelve signatories and, as so often in later years, one "Anon." In this case, the name is known. It was that of William Staughton, at that time a theological student, and later, in America, a founder of the American Baptist Missionary Convention. Carey's name did not appear in the list, but the profits on the *Enquiry* had already been promised by him towards the venture. The receptacle for this offering was Andrew Fuller's snuff box (still in the Society's possession), the embossed lid of which portrays the conversion of Saul of Tarsus. This first B.M.S. offering, totalling £13 2s. 6d., raised the ridicule and scorn of Sydney Smith, but it proved to be the beginning of an ever increasing river of support. Andrew Fuller was appointed Secretary—a position he held till his death in May 1815 at the age of sixty-two. Reynold Hogg was made Treasurer (he resigned in 1795 in favour of a layman), and these two, together with William Carey, John Sutcliff, and Ryland (frequently Chairman), were constituted the Society's first committee (now a body of one-hundred-and-twenty-four elected, thirty-eight honorary, and forty *ex-officio* members). A typical remark of the new Secretary, Andrew Fuller, must be quoted. It was addressed to Sutcliff and Ryland: "You excel me in wisdom especially in foreseeing difficulties. I therefore want to advise with you both, but to execute without you." Kettering, therefore, as the venue of the decisive meeting, was the birthplace of the Baptist Missionary Society and of the world missionary movement. Moulton had seen the birth of the idea; Leicester had launched the *Enquiry*; the "Deathless Sermon" had been preached at Nottingham. Widow Wallis's house, however, was in Kettering; Fuller was a Kettering pastor and Kettering became Fuller's office as Secretary of the newly formed Society. Fuller did his best throughout his life to keep the Society's Headquarters at Kettering, warning all concerned not to let the Society fall into the hands of the counting-house people in London. In the meantime, from Kettering and the Northamptonshire Association, the good news travelled of this decisive action, and good news travelled back again to Kettering of interest and support. From Birmingham "the surprising sum of £70" was quickly subscribed through the effective leadership of Samuel Pearce, to whom the mission field made a strong personal appeal. Scotland, Fuller found to his joy, was ready to respond to appeals he made in person. Yorkshire was stirred among both laymen and ministers, including John Fawcett, whom Carey met. The West, led by Ryland, of Bristol, also responded nobly. The Baptist leaders of the Metropolis, however, were slower in their support. The ancient Dr. Stennett, all too conscious that here was a country minister's scheme, played the part of a Gamaliel as he bade the ministers of London hold aloof. This advice, with one or two exceptions, they accepted for quite a time. In later years, however, the situation changed most happily, with London carrying a lion's share of the responsibility. It was Benjamin Beddome, of Bourton, however, who voiced the objection that will always be heard whenever an appeal is made for work overseas. Speaking for so many others

down the years as well as for himself, he declared in
effect that charity should begin at home. Actually Carey
was a personal disappointment to him. He had wanted
him, "the most suitable person in the kingdom," to be
his own successor, and now his plan had come to
naught. Carey was destined for elsewhere.

V. The Volunteer

So HERE WAS a Missionary Society, newly formed but without any missionaries, a home organization without any foreign representatives. But this was not long to be the case. At the fourth meeting of this little group, the same William Carey, married and with a growing family, shoemaker and pastor, writer of the *Enquiry* and preacher of the "Deathless Sermon," offered himself for service overseas. The "Go ye therefore . . .", the never to be abrogated command of his Lord, had become "Go thou . . ." The logic of his own arguments demanded that he should declare "Here am I, send me." But he was not to go alone, for already at the third meeting of the Society, when the agenda included the all-important item as to where the Society should find "the most promising openings," a letter was read from William Carey (for some reason absent from the gathering), commending to his colleagues a ship's surgeon, a certain John Thomas, described by Carey as the "Bengal Missionary." As a "one-man missionary society," he was seeking to raise funds so that he might return to Bengal, India, where he had already spent some five or six years. This same John Thomas had been converted by Dr. Stennett in London and baptized by Rev. Abraham Booth. Carey declared himself in favour of uniting the two financial endeavours into one fund, with Bengal in mind in the first instance and with a larger plan in the background for future development in other regions, for example Tahiti or West Africa. He had been attracted to the South Seas as a mission field from the earliest days, and the thrilling narratives of Captain Cook's voyages and in particular the story of his tragic death, had stimulated and deepened his concern for a primitive people unable to escape any longer from Western associations. Also, West Africa as the scene of the dreadful raids of the slave traders had long been on his mind and conscience. Thanks to the arrival of John Thomas on the scene, however, and "his glowing descriptions of Bengal," it was India which became the first Baptist Missionary Society field. "We saw that there was a gold mine in India," said Andrew Fuller, reporting on this historic session at a later date, "and that it was as deep as the centre of the earth. We asked, Who will venture to explore it? I will venture to go down, replied Carey, but remember you (addressing Fuller, Sutcliff and Ryland) must hold the ropes." They solemnly agreed to do so, promising "Never while we live shall we desert him." In view of the weakness of character that Thomas afterwards displayed, and his volatile temperament, and particularly with the arrangements for sailing on the *Earl of Oxford* breaking down through Thomas's debts, it was surprising that two such shrewd and solid men as Carey and Fuller should have allowed themselves to be persuaded of the fitness of such a man, however eloquent and full of zeal, to accompany Carey overseas. The debts he had contracted in India, the extent of which he disclosed quite candidly to the committee, together with his erratic behaviour there, had driven his influential friends to repudiate him and later to decline to support the mission because of his connection with it. Later, Carey was to say of him that he was "a man of sterling worth but perhaps the most singular make of any man on earth." Nevertheless, although in many ways a liability, he had his place in the scheme of God's appointing, and it was because of his experience of the climate and languages, peoples and religions of India, that the B.M.S. first turned to that great sub-continent with its citadels of Hinduism, its Buddhism in its original habitat, and its Mohammedanism with a multitude of mosques. It was also largely because of the medical skill of John Thomas in dealing with a dislocated shoulder that the first convert, Krishna Pal, was won to faith in Jesus Christ.

It was on the 10th January 1793, in Kettering, that William Carey and John Thomas were first appointed missionaries "to the East Indies for preaching the Gospel to the heathen." The finances of the infant Society, which at this stage was courageously undertaking considerable expense, showed some £130 available for the initial team of two men, their wives and the family of Carey. This was altogether fantastic when thought of in connection with the wealth of the East India Company, the profits quickly made by its servants for the Company and the fortunes they made all the more quickly for themselves. It was with good reason that the term "Nabob" came into common use. Carey and Thomas were to have £100 or £150 per annum for the whole party until they could support themselves, and, as things worked out, in the first three years the total sum sent them was £200. The passage money came to hand as the result of tours by Carey and John Thomas. Some of it was raised by Andrew Fuller as he began to lay the foundations of itineration that made him something of a later rival to John Wesley.

It was on a tour made by Carey in Yorkshire that the circle began to widen as another recruit emerged in Hull, William Ward the printer, to whom Carey said, "If the Lord blesses us, we shall want a person of your business to enable us to print scriptures. I hope you will come after us." And this he did in 1799. The Valedictory Service of Carey and Thomas, recalling the setting apart of Barnabas and Paul at Antioch for the first missionary journey of all, took place in Carey's Church at Harvey Lane, Leicester, on 20th March 1793, in the chapel that had had to be enlarged to accommodate the growing company of those wishing to hear Carey preach Sunday by Sunday. In two years, also, the membership had doubled. There were no fewer than three sermons, the first preached by Thomas with references to idolators, the second by the Treasurer of the Society, though not on finance, and the third by Fuller on "The objects you must keep in view, the directions you must observe, the difficulties you must encounter and the reward you may expect," a sermon that often cheered and rallied Carey in days to come. In the Harvey Lane Minute Book there was a rather laconic reference to this notable event. It reads, "Sep. Oct. Nov. Dec. Jan. no business of importance except that in Jan. our pastor gave us notice that he should leave us in March, having engaged to go on a Mission to Bengal in the East Indies." Thus inauspiciously, so it would seem, the great venture was launched.

Part II

LIFE IN INDIA

I. The First Experiment

WHEN CAREY AND his family and John Thomas disembarked from the *Krön Princessa Maria* at Calcutta on 11th November 1793, the arrival of this pathetic-looking party went unheeded. Europe was concerned with Napoleon; England was surrendering to reaction; the East India Company was busy with its lucrative trade, and the vast Indian population was sunk in its age-long apathy. Because they arrived in a Danish ship, their entry into India was not a matter of close investigation by the officials of the Company. No one took any notice. There was no welcoming party with garlands and songs as would happen today. "I am scarcely perceived among the millions of Bengalis," said Carey of himself later. But it must have been immediately apparent to a keen-eyed observer, if there had been any such about, that a new personal force had arrived in the East to challenge the ancient faiths. How Carey longed to begin at once, without any waiting or hesitation, his life-work of Christian witness, but this was impossible, despite the lessons in Bengali he had had on board the ship from John Thomas. As an immediate first step he employed Ram Basu, one of John Thomas's inquirers, none too secure in his faith, as his interpreter and pundit. His first thought was not the vivid scene, not the sacred river, not the strange buildings, but the masses of the people. It was for them that he had come, and for them only.

Financial difficulties, however, soon began to be pressing, largely owing to John Thomas's optimistic attitude. The goods Carey and he had brought, valued at £150, by the sale of which they were to pay their way, realized far less than had been anticipated. Carey said rather ruefully of John Thomas that he was only fit to live at sea, where both his daily work and needs would be ordered for him. Because of these troubles, the party made the experiment of moving thirty miles from Calcutta to Bandel, a Portuguese settlement on the River Hooghli, where they proposed to "live like the natives." Nearby was one of the most ancient Hindu centres, Nuddea, the birthplace of Chaitanya, the mystic, and formerly a royal city, which offered to Carey a magnificent base of operations of a frontal kind. But it was not to be, for there was no land available for him to cultivate.

So Carey returned to Calcutta without a house and with a wife mentally ill, and with other members of the family physically indisposed after the squalid weeks at Bandel. He was just too late in applying for a post with the Botanic Gardens, a post for which his life-long interest in flowers, plants and trees and a botanical monograph already produced, sufficiently qualified him. His subsequent services to these very Gardens will be described later. Then just when he had failed in his attempt to work in a garden there came the suggestion that he might attempt the jungle. With this in view, he hired a boat with borrowed money and took his slow, plodding progress to the Soondarbans in the Ganges delta. There he built a bamboo house on a plot of a few acres, rent free for three years, in the midst of tiger-haunted swamps with wild buffalo and pig in the neighbourhood and a crocodile in a pond only ten yards

Carey's pulpit at Serampore.

Rev. J. B. Middlebrook standing by the bust of Carey in the Botanical Gardens, Calcutta.

from the door. Here he sought to be a farmer. Shades of the countryside long ago in Paulerspury! At this time he wrote in a letter, "I am in a strange land, alone, with no Christian friend, a large family and nothing to support their needs." But in a letter home he roundly declared, "I would not renounce my undertaking for all the world."

But there came an invitation which changed his place of occupation and residence. Through connections with John Thomas, a certain Mr. G. Udny offered Thomas and Carey posts as managers to take charge of his new indigo factories in the district of Malda in North Bengal. The posts each carried a salary of £250 a year, with commission and a share in ownership. Carey at once accepted this "providential" invitation and moved to Mudnabati in June 1794. He wrote at once to Fuller to say that he would no longer require financial help from the Society. The committee replied in Fuller's absence, and much to Carey's surprise and, indeed, to his chagrin, warning him against what would now be called "the profit motive." In fact he was also setting aside one-third of his income for mission purposes. He received a licence from the Company as an indigo planter for at least five years, and immediately applied himself to his new occupation with all his customary concentration and desire for mastery. But unfortunately the siting of the factory was thoroughly bad for both Europeans and natives. Peter Carey died of dysentery at the age of five, and there was a pitiful struggle with India's caste system before a grave could be dug and the small, pathetic body carried to it. Mrs. Carey's condition of mind deteriorated severely. Carey himself was at death's door with fever, and his principal helpers were most of them sick and ill. But he rejoiced in the opportunity

C

that indigo planting gave him of fulfilling the vocation
that had brought him from England to India.

With this in view, also he sought to manage the
factory on Christian principles, setting his face, for
example, against anything in the shape of bribery. His
duties kept him busy only three months of the year, and
that in the rainy season. The remainder of his time he
was able to devote to his master-passion, and quite soon
the pattern of his life to its very end began to declare
itself. Inevitably the preacher in him also took every
opportunity. His district covered some twenty square
miles, comprising two hundred villages, with five hundred people working at the factory. In the event of
converts losing caste, he hoped to employ them himself.
It was his custom to travel in two small boats and to
walk ten to twenty miles from village to village. The
present writer can testify both to the cramped quarters
of an even larger boat than Carey had, the *Dipti
Dut* (Messenger of Light) in the same district, and to
the evangelistic opportunity such a mode of travel
affords.

It was not till 1806, however, that any of the native
inquirers in this region became declared converts. In the
meantime, therefore, idolatry continued to maintain its
unbroken front. Among the Europeans and Eurasians a
small Baptist Church was formed in March 1795, the
first in Bengal. Then also, in the field of translation,
Carey, as was his habit, was writing down every new
word as he heard it. He was listening to his children
as they prattled with Indian children. He was grappling
with the difficulty of using the meagre spoken Bengali
of the people as the vehicle of biblical truth. He was
to be found arranging for each newly translated portion
of scripture to be read to crowds of natives to see what

they could make of it. Already he had begun to prepare a grammar and dictionary of the Bengali language, but he had discovered that his hopes of mastery of the Bengali language depended upon a close knowledge of Sanskrit. With his customary industry and courage, he soon gained an expert knowledge of the grammar, vocabulary and literature of this basic language, and at once his Bengali translations were greatly enriched in variety and depth. The Bengali New Testament was speedily made ready for printing.

At this time, also, a wooden press was purchased in Calcutta for £40, and, cutting his own types, Carey printed the Gospel of Mark. So great was his enthusiasm for this machine, and so close his devotion to it, that there were those who said that at last they had discovered the Englishman's idol! Nor were schools left out of the picture, and these early experiments carried the germs of his later activities in this field. He gathered forty boys, some of them orphans, into a school with the number thus limited for economic reasons. Carey hoped to replace apathy with questioning and to make these lads curious far beyond the usual Bengali level. Then, also, with John Thomas, the doctor, at hand in Dinajpur (where his grave can be visited), it was more than likely that something would be done for the suffering and diseased population. Carey pleaded for free medicines from home. The missionaries had to be their own doctors and their neighbours' also. They were surrounded by "wretched afflicted folk," and John Thomas's house, some sixteen miles to the north, often bore resemblance to the spectacle at Capernaum when at eventide the sick and ill were gathered round our Lord. It was during this early six-year period that Carey first saw the burning of a widow, and by his urgent expostulations with the relatives ran dangerous personal risks.

And so a full-scale missionary programme began to be worked out in Dinajpur. Its characteristics were preaching, teaching and translation, and it was already marked by a far-reaching strategy. Here was the future Serampore in embryo. The Greek myth of Minerva, the goddess of wisdom, springing fully grown from the brain of her father, Jupiter, comes to mind in relation to this rather prosaic Englishman in the India of the eighteenth century. He began as he continued, and he ended with the same full force. He manifested an immediate maturity. Carey said of Dinajpur, "I could not easily have a more eligible site for the Mission." Writing home he said of it, also, "A more proper spot to make a large stand for the spread of the Gospel could scarcely have been chosen. This is a situation so central . . . that, had we sufficient men and a proper plan, the Gospel might with ease and small expense be sent from hence through all Hindoostan, Persia, Boutan, Assam and . . ." further afield. Writing also in another letter, he declared that Dinajpur was a place where "all necessary languages may be learned."

The situation, therefore, was full of promise, yet nevertheless there was a fundamental difficulty. Well known as he was to magistrates, judges and others as a preacher, and ready to avow himself as a missionary on all levels of society, he was well aware that to be included in this category by the East India Company could only mean expulsion as an "interloper." This greatly chafed his spirit, and his long visit to the Bhootans in the North for purposes connected with the indigo business, with the welcome he and John Thomas received as Christian "Lamas," the freedom they were accorded, the readiness of the people to hear, and their sympathetic response, made him contemplate leaving the indigo factory and staking all on a missionary venture in this more northerly region under the shadow of stupendous mountain ranges. He was all the more tempted to do this since his first new colleague, the republican-minded John Fountain, also from the Midlands, had been refused a licence as his assistant on arrival in 1796. To continue in Dinajpur would mean working entirely alone, with no hope of fellow-missionaries at his side. There could never be the kind of team that he desired so strongly, and that was later the characteristic of Serampore.

It was at this time, when at least one alternative base of operations was in Carey's mind, that Mr. Udny decided to return to England, abandoning his indigo business with its unsatisfactory economic returns. Thus, at the age of thirty-eight, Carey, despite his developing programme of a basic missionary kind, was precariously placed. Nevertheless, if he had died at this time, his fundamental plans as already revealed, and his typical methods as already practised, would have provided future generations with at least the outline of his later achievements at Serampore.

But Dinajpur was not the end. New decisions were speedily asked of him, and the answer he gave and its wonderful consequences, as he said years later, were "the means of preserving the Mission."

II. Serampore, 1800-1834

DURING THIS CRISIS, and to his very great surprise, Carey suddenly saw approaching him one Sunday morning, William Ward, the printer and newspaper editor whom he had last seen in London at the Monument. There was therefore no need of any such words of introduction as H. M. Stanley addressed to David Livingstone when they met in Africa. It was a decisive encounter, decisive for the whole future of missions in India and the East.

Ward had arrived with Joshua and Hannah Marshman. Joshua Marshman hailed from Wiltshire and then from Bristol, while Mrs. Marshman was a Bristolian. With them also had come Brunsdon and Grant, members of Ryland's Church, Bristol. They had made the voyage in an American vessel, the *Criterion*, by Fuller's arrangements, and, as happily advised by Charles Grant, a director of the East India Company, they had proceeded to the Danish settlement of Fredericksnagore, known in British circles as Serampore. Even so, they had difficulties with the British authorities who were so close at hand. They had been described in the press, unfortunately, as "Papists," not as "Baptists," and, with the fear of French spies very much in the minds of the authorities, they were regarded with the utmost suspicion. Ward, on his part, also had his moment of surprise, for he noted that Carey, though rather stouter, was still a young man. One can readily imagine Carey's eager interest in all that Ward could tell him both of news from home and of the situation they had met as a missionary party on arrival. In the discussions that followed, a basic decision was taken that made Serampore one of the most famous places in the world as the cradle of modern missions. Carey quickly saw the force of Ward's arguments, and he delighted in the prospect of being able openly, without jeopardizing his work and opportunities, to declare himself a missionary. Freedom to work in Danish territory would also help, so he said, "to make our designs well understood by the English Government nearby," and indeed, this eventually turned out to be the case. He was reluctant, also, having to forego Ward as his colleague in the whole work of printing. Such a relationship would be forbidden in Dinajpur. Ward had only been able to meet Carey there because he was armed with a Danish passport. The Danish authorities "had extended their patronage and support to Lutheran missionaries, men like Ziegenbalg, Schultze, Fabricius and Schwartz, in the South of India." Serampore could also be the nucleus of an abiding missionary fellowship, though evidently the Moravians had found it necessary to withdraw from this area some years before. Also its numerous inhabitants offered an immediate field for evangelism, as its location offered a strategic centre for all the further purposes Carey had in mind. So Dinajpur, with its missionary beginnings, its church and inquirers, and its school, was left for later development, such indigo business as there was being abandoned. How typical it was of Carey that on the way to Serampore he sought to evangelize such aboriginal tribes as the Santals, with their beliefs in evil spirits, little thinking at the time that success among them later would be one of the glorious triumphs of the Gospel. So Carey came to Serampore on the 10th January 1800. After a somewhat chequered start, he was now set fair on a lasting course, never to be interrupted even by a visit home to England. In fact, already in letters home he was telling the church at Leicester and also his friend, Samuel Pearce, that he did not anticipate seeing them again. At Serampore he joined William Ward ("a great prize"), and Joshua Marshman ("a prodigy of diligence and prudence") and his wife Hannah, the first woman missionary to India. They have been described as "a trio of missionary heroes and geniuses to which it would be impossible to present a parallel." Carey and the Marshmans were to remain together for over thirty years. Ward died of cholera in 1823. During this long period, there were many other changes. Fountain, returning to Dinajpur, died there in 1800. Grant and Brunsdon died in the very early days, the former within less than three weeks, the latter within twelve months, and there was much coming and going as, during the years, new missionaries arrived and moved out to other places. Ward married Fountain's widow, formerly a Miss Tidd. The first Mrs. Carey died in 1807 after many years of mental distress, the second Mrs. Carey, Lady Rumohr, a Danish woman, died in 1821, while the third Mrs. Carey outlived her husband by a few years.

The decision of the five families to live together on a corporate basis, even sharing a common table for meals, with no one engaged in private profit and all pooling their financial returns, owed its success to the character and spirit of the foundation members of the group. The common fund thus created was "to be applied at the will of the majority to the support of their

respective families, of the cause of God around them
and of the widow and family of such as might be removed by death." Carey, as usual, was the moving
spirit, and the *Enquiry* may be quoted as suggesting a
first draft of a shared economy. Also, in a letter to
Fuller, he mentioned the Moravians as having pioneered
along these lines. At a later date, he said, "If we give
up the resolution which was formed on the subject of
private trade when we first united at Serampore, the
mission is from that hour a lost cause." It is not easy
to understand this conviction of Carey's regarding the
fate of the mission. One can appreciate that this pattern
of community life would result in certain financial
economies; it would provide for an organized distribution of labour and, indeed, also it might be a measure
of witness of Christian brotherhood to non-Christians
in the vicinity. But it would never have been possible
to work such a scheme without continuity in the
original circle. Carey, Marshman and Ward, in the
providence of God, were given long enough together
to make the experiment successfully, but the longer
they were together in such closeness of personal and
social, financial and spiritual, intimacy, the more difficult it must have been, as proved to be the case, for
younger men to join them. In the event, of course, the
whole missionary movement has swung away from this
Serampore pattern, missionaries being supported directly
from their home bases. Unlike the Moravians, "Serampore" had no officially appointed head of its composite
family, the superintendents of its affairs being in
monthly rotation, with Carey as Treasurer and Fountain the first Librarian. Mrs. Marshman's household
books give valuable details of the economics and economies of the time. They drew up a "Form of Agree-

ment" which, with its subsequent revisions in the light
of experience, never lost its original character and it
was never challenged from within. The tragic story of
breakdown in an earlier example of community life, as
reported in Acts, Chapter 5, and as represented by
Ananias and Sapphira, was not repeated at Serampore.
The original income was supplied by London, and this
was increasingly supplemented by the profits on the
Press and the fees from the schools and, later, as will
be seen, by Carey's professorial salary. Finance at
Serampore was never a chronic difficulty, though the
collapse of the great business and banking houses in
Calcutta between 1830 and 1833 brought disaster to the
missionary group. Their first important transaction was
the acquisition by purchase of a large house at a cost of
£800; rents, as Carey had anticipated, being much too
high for a tenancy to be contemplated. This amount,
which was quickly advanced by the Society, was repaid
in a very few years, and further properties were added
and paid for. All this property (which was to be a later
bone of contention) was vested in the B.M.S. with themselves as trustees. The most serious modification of the
original "Form of Agreement" resulted from personal
family responsibilities. The members of the group had
relatives in England with increasingly impaired health
and sometimes in straitened circumstances. There was
also each individual's responsibility for providing for
his widow and children. It was therefore agreed that
one-tenth should be deducted by each contributor "from
the nett product of his labour," the fund so created to
be in the private hands of the individual concerned.

A word or two should be said about the siting of the
Mission base at Serampore, almost an ideal location. The
immediate reason for the Ward and Marshman party

landing at Serampore was, of course, that there they
came under the protection of the Danish flag and were
outside the jurisdiction of the hostile East India Company. As declared missionaries, hiding nothing of their
evangelistic intentions, they were welcomed by the
Governor, Colonel Bie, who expressed the hope that
their number would be added to. He attended worship
in their house on the very first Sunday after their arrival,
William Ward preaching on this occasion from the
courageous words of Acts 20. 24. At Serampore they
remained undisturbed even during the brief hostilities
between England and Denmark, when Serampore fell
into British hands. Moreover, in 1845, when the East
India Company purchased Tranquebar and Serampore
from Denmark, the rights of Serampore College were
re-affirmed. At Serampore, therefore, security of tenure
was achieved and the precarious element happily removed. Serampore was only fourteen miles from
Calcutta, a proximity the value of which was capital-
ized by trading companies with their factories along the
River Hooghli. Each successive wave of traders—Portuguese, Dutch, French, English and Danish—chose to
enter the neighbourhood of Serampore, with its increasing density of population, its facilities as a port and its
concentration of keen and intelligent Bengalis. It was
also, in its way, a cave of Adullam, a sanctuary for
debtors and wastrels. It was Ward who said, "Being near
to Calcutta . . . is of the utmost importance to our
School, our Press and our connection with England."
The Serampore trio saw Serampore as the strategic
centre for the evangelism of India as a whole and for
eastern regions beyond.

This area was also a centre of Hindu worship in its
more degrading and terrible forms. Nuddea had earlier

found favour with both Carey on the spot and Fuller in England as the focal point of the Mission because it was "the centre of Brahmanical superstition and Sanskrit learning." Its abandonment in favour of Serampore did not mean that the Mission had removed itself from the horrors of idolatry. Serampore was only second to Puri as the shrine of Juggernaut worship, with its annual festival of the newly built wooden car taking the god and goddess to their summer residence and with the annual toll of lives as devotees flung themselves beneath the wheels. Also at hand was the shrine of Tarakeswar, with its multitudes of pilgrims (including many widows) who made their painful progress by measuring their length along the road. Even now, at the time of writing, there is a Hindu temple almost at the gates of Serampore, and there are also many Muslims in the town and area with their distinctive beliefs and buildings, rites and customs. Serampore, therefore, was in the forefront of the battle with ancient rivals of the Gospel and furnished an excellent base, in the language of the time, for "assaults on the fortress of Satan."

Ward's journal allows for the reconstruction of an average day in the life of the Serampore group, and the relevant portion reads as follows:

"About six o'clock we rise; brother Carey to his garden; brother Marshman to his school at seven; brother Brunsdon, Felix and I, to the printing-office. At eight, the bell rings for family worship: we assemble in the hall; sing, read and pray. Breakfast. Afterwards brother Carey goes to the translation, or reading proofs: brother Marshman to school, and the rest to the printing office. Our compositor having left us, we do without: we print three half-sheets of 2,000 each in a week; have five pressmen, one folder, and one binder. At twelve o'clock we take a luncheon; then most of us shave and bathe, read and sleep before dinner, which we have at three. After dinner we deliver our thoughts on a text or question : this we find to be very profitable. Brother and sister Marshman keep their schools till after two. In the afternoon, if business be done in the office, I read and try to talk Bengali with the brammhan. We drink tea about seven, and have little or no supper. We have Bengali preaching once or twice in the week, and on Thursday evening we have an experience meeting. On Saturday evening we meet to compose differences and transact business, after prayer, which is always immediately after tea. Felix is very useful in the office; William goes to school, and part of the day learns to bind. We meet two hours before breakfast on the first Monday in the month, and each one prays for the salvation of the Bengal heathen. At night we unite our prayers for the universal spread of the Gospel."

In this diary of a typical day, Ward indicates as will have been seen, some of the inner workings of the Serampore brotherhood. He tells of experience meetings, discussions of scripture texts, the weekly effort to iron out personal difficulties and the regulated duties and responsibilities of the various members of the group. How clearly he reveals in action the spiritual sanctions and ideals of the community and its members as set out in the "Agreement" drawn up in 1805 and which it was suggested should be read in all the mission stations three times a year on a Sunday. In this document, after referring to the example of Brainerd as a man of fervent prayer, and referring also to the qualities needed by missionaries, there is to be found the following moving and effective appeal :

"Finally, let us give ourselves unreservedly to this

glorious cause. Let us never think that our time, our gifts, our strength, our families, or even the clothes we wear are our own. Let us sanctify them all to God and His cause."

What a wonderful fulfilment of the promise of Christ concerning the two or three gathered together in His Name (Matthew 18. 20). But this description by Ward also outlines the activities that characterized Serampore from the very first day and which remained throughout the long years the main endeavour. They were Bible translation, the work of education, all that has to do with printing, together with preaching and intercession. The following chapters will occupy themselves with these various interests as they found achievement and even triumph. Preaching was blessed in 1800 with the first of Indian converts, followed by the gathering of converts into churches. Translation, aided by the printing press, issued the first complete Bengali New Testament in 1801. Education was developed in a great variety of its branches, and as early as 1801 Carey joined the staff of the Fort William College. Then in 1818 the Serampore College prospectus was issued, and shortly afterwards the noble pile of buildings was erected. Missionary strategy based on Serampore soon developed into a network of stations. By 1805, Carey was suggesting interdenominational conferences at the Cape of Good Hope. Direct action by Carey in social reform, particularly the first steps towards securing the forbidding of the burning of widows, was quickly in evidence, and this was before 1805. Also, from the day the property was purchased, he had begun to create his lovely garden with its trees, shrubs and flowers, and then as the years went by, with his own slowly plodding feet, he made "Carey's Walk." Thus the lines of action which were developed at Serampore over thirty years were laid down very early and, indeed, most of the decisive dates came at the very beginning of the period. In the chapters that follow, the story is taken to Carey's death in 1834 and his main activities as preacher, educationalist and translator, man of conscience and compassion and missionary strategist, are successively defined and described in their motive, range and goal.

Part III

HIS LIFE AND WORK

I. *The Preacher*

IN THE LONG HISTORY of the Christian Church, it is necessary to go back to Mars' Hill and the Apostle Paul's witness to his faith in Athens to find a relevant parallel to Carey's preaching at Serampore as soon as he arrived. Immediately he had been presented to the Danish Governor on the 11th January 1800, "he went out and preached to the natives." One wonders what his hearers thought about him as they halted in the busy street, rose up from the pavement which was their only home, or paused on the way to temple, shrine or mosque. Their surprise must have been great as they heard this stocky Englishman speaking so fluently in Bengali, and their wonder must have grown when they discovered that his theme was religious. Nothing further removed from a mud-smeared holy man, a fakir in strange contortions, a Sadhu with an abstracted gaze or a Buddhist priest in his saffron robes, could have been imagined than this European with his ordinary look and his neat but undistinguished garb.

Yet he represented, though none of them realized it, a religious challenge fashioned not in his own country nor in the West but in the East, in ancient Palestine. It was a challenge that presented Jesus Christ as the only Redeemer in a land where "not one soul thinks of God aright." There was none other Name than His under heaven whereby men might be saved. This title "Redeemer" was used by Carey of his Lord more frequently in his *Enquiry* than any other. He used it often in his correspondence, and among his contemporaries Fuller, Ryland and others it seems to have been the identifying description. But in a letter to Samuel Pearce in 1796 he wrote, "I generally set forth Jesus as the Saviour . . . though the immediate subject be what it may." In a further letter he spoke of "Jesus Christ the great fountain and herald of salvation." Then again, of the primitive Paharis he said, "I have a strong persuasion that the doctrine of a dying Saviour would, under the Holy Spirit's influence, melt their hearts." How he rejoiced when he could say, as early as 1795, "The name of Jesus Christ is no longer strange in this neighbourhood."

Like the ancient prophets, he had a fire burning in his bones. "I feel," he said, "a burning desire that all the world may know." Like the first apostles, he knew the agony of "Woe is me if I preach not the Gospel." As a youthful local preacher in Northamptonshire with his "crude" sermons, as he later described them, and then as a settled minister in Moulton and Leicester, it was always his joy to preach the word of God. It was when Andrew Fuller heard him preach in Northampton that he grasped Carey's hand when he was leaving the pulpit and expressed the hope that they would come to know each other better. It was his sermon at Nottingham, with its great slogan "Expect and Attempt" that, as James Culross said, "created the Baptist Missionary Society." With this background then as a preacher, how chafed he was at the frustrating silence during his first year or so in India when, as he had to confess, he could not preach as yet except to his own family. How tantalizing it was to have to stand wordless at John Thomas's side in the first days in Calcutta. How gladly

D

he took advantage of his growing command of Bengali, mixed with Hindustani, to preach, however haltingly, for half an hour to his employees in the indigo factory. How he rejoiced when at last in Serampore he could go out and preach understandably to the crowds, with his longing to know enough of the language of the country to preach Christ to the natives fulfilled at last. How feelingly, and indeed how courageously, in his address to the brilliant gathering in the new Government House presided over by the Governor-General in 1804, he referred to his habit of preaching to the multitudes daily. On another occasion he recalled how the inhabitants of Calcutta used to stand "in a thick-wedged crowd for hours together in the heat of a Bengali summer" and how they used "to hang on our lips." In his seventieth year it could still be said of him that he took his turn in preaching both in Bengali and English. Preaching remained his master-passion to the end, though, as later chapters will show, his ministry was wider than preaching and the desk and the fields claimed him as well as the pulpit.

There is an interesting description of Carey as a preacher from the pen of his nephew, Eustace, in which he says that his uncle chose "plain, elementary subjects. He found them in the life of his own spirit. He never imagined that they could be exhausted or trite. He gave them an easy, natural treatment with no excursiveness. He had no great variety or range in his illustrations. He was neither imaginative nor poetical." As supporting this view the elder Robert Hall had said to him once, "There are no 'likes' in your sermons," referring probably to our Lord's practice in his parables of commencing with the phrase, "The Kingdom of God is like . . ." Carey's preaching was described nevertheless by both

Marshman and certain visitors to Serampore as "lively" and "animated," and on the occasion of the Deathless Sermon, Ryland spoke of "the sluice gates of the preacher's soul opening."

It would be both profitable and instructive for research to be made into the place Carey gave comparatively to primitive animists and to Mohammedans and Buddhists in his long-continued missionary campaign. In a letter to his father in 1793 he wrote, "I am appointed to go to Bengal in the East Indies, a missionary to the Hindoos." As the ship off Calcutta sighted the shore and the coconut groves, his cry was, "O may my heart be prepared for our work, and the kingdom of Christ be set up among the poor Hindoos." This seems to suggest that it was the Hindu with his philosophy and theology, his sacred books and age-long worship, his idolatry and terrible social practices, on whom his sights were trained. But his mission could never be exclusive, and in the Leicester minute book it was described in general terms as "a Mission to the East Indies." Fuller, writing in England about the same time, spoke of "rescuing poor heathens and Mohammedans from under Satan's yoke." There are records of his movements among such primitive tribes as the Khasis and of his hopes of their conversion, hopes reaped so marvellously in later generations not only among the Khasis but among the Santals, the Lushais, Konds and others. Indeed, it would have been strange if the missionary with Tahiti first in mind had been blind and deaf to the people who in India "were without caste, priests, or public religion." Buddhists also attracted his evangelistic concern as was evident from the contact and fellowship he had with the Bhooteas in the Darjeeling area during his indigo period. There are also frequent references to Mohammedans in his journals and letters. Such sentences occur as "Spoke a word or two to a Mohammedan upon the things of God" and "I now rejoice in seeing a regular congregation . . . Mussulmans and Brahmans and other classes of Hindus." He also declared that "a more general attack upon the heathen world should be made—and the Mohammedan world too," and of North Bengal he said, "Here is certainly a large field of usefulness; much larger than you can conceive, both among Hindoos and Mussulmen." He and Thomas in 1795 were contemplating a College for twelve boys—six Mohammedans and six Hindus. In the first Periodical Accounts he reported gladly that he could not "perceive anything unfriendly in the conduct of the Mohammedans," though, as he said elsewhere, the Moors were more rigid and fierce than the Hindus. It was a tract published at Serampore in Persian containing some slighting remarks on Mohammed and Mohammedans "that precipitated a crisis with the Government authorities." Fortunately, once it was established that the offending strictures had been included by a native translator from Bengali into Persian, entirely without authority, everything worked out advantageously. But the Mission had come perilously near being put out of action by the authorities. He rejoiced in the first Mohammedan convert, Peroo, as the beginning of the victory over that same Islam to which so many of the lands listed in his *Enquiry* had had to be assigned. How fitting it was that Mohammedans as well as Hindus lined the route to his grave in 1834. Then in a letter home we find his longing poignantly expressed that the members of the Society at home along "with many, many English" may meet "in the worlds of light" with "many, many Hindus and Muslims."

But it was the Hindus who were his main objective. His concern with Sanskrit, the bulk of his translations, his mission strategy along the Ganges and his plans for Serampore College, would almost have been pointless if it had not been that he was seeking to understand and indeed to undermine Hinduism and to win its adherents to the truth as it is in Jesus Christ. Like Ezekiel, in his vision (Chapter VIII), looking in on the altars and sun-worshippers in Jerusalem and like the Apostle Paul in Athens as he saw a city given over to idolatry, Carey was shocked to the core in a paroxysm of revulsion, at the sight of India's idolatry with all its blasphemy, obsceneness and cruelty. He spoke also from time to time of its "lightheartedness" in relation to feasts and festivals. He proclaimed the one God, not the Allah of Islam, not any one of the Hindu gods, not the ultimate Brahman, nor even "the great object of worship who could only be seen by the mind," but the Father of Jesus Christ in whom God was revealed in His true identity and His Incarnate fulness. As he faced the idolatry of India he took heart as he recalled the triumph of Christ centuries before over the gods of Greece and Rome and of Britain. He also spoke of many who were by no means friendly to the Gospel who were prepared to predict the spreading of Christianity throughout the country and the downfall of their own ways of worship.

Though it was Carey who gave Hinduism translations of its ancient books, he did so not because of their religious and moral value but in order that their weaknesses, absurdities and limitations might be revealed. He declared at Mudnabati that he had "never yet met with a Hindu who was proof against the absurdities of his own Shasters." Of his hearers he demanded conversion, a new birth in Christ through the power of the Holy

Spirit. They were to turn from the "grossness of idolatry to serve the true and living God." He was no syncretist seeking a blending of faiths. He never presented Christianity as the crown of Hinduism nor did he acknowledge it to be a preparatory stage to the Gospel, an equivalent in its own way of the Old Testament. Nevertheless, even in his *Enquiry*, he spoke of converted peoples "contributing by their preachings and writings to the glory of our Redeemer's name." It was sin that was the radical human problem and not destiny as the Hindus declared. He called men and women to repentance, to break with anything that could not be called the mind and will of Christ, to surrender themselves to the spirit of the living Lord who had died for them on Calvary, to join His Church and to seek His will for communities and themselves. Later he spoke of "disseminating the humane and saving principles of the Christian religion," and in the *Enquiry* he had referred to "universal benevolence and genuine philanthropy." He refers to "millions of perishing heathens tormented in this life by idolatry, superstition and ignorance and exposed to miseries in the world to come." Hell fire was never mentioned by him in the *Enquiry*, nor was the fear of it conspicuous in his preaching as a basis of appeal. In Carey's view, evangelism, while seeking the salvation of the individual soul and the way of life in Christ, must be made aware of the importance of society and the things that hold it together, give it significance and grace and form its traditions and culture. He actually wrote, "Would not the spread of the Gospel be the most effectual means of their civilization?" Not only must people be delivered from the bondage of heathenism, they must be given the opportunity of entering a richer and fuller life. In the *Enquiry* it is clear that the Christianity he proclaimed meant the end of brutishness and savagery and the coming of civilization.

Carey needed all his patience as he was called upon to wait for as long as seven years before any of his Indian hearers testified firmly to conversion. There had been many false starts which had raised his hopes, but no one had persevered. One young man had declared in words that carry a New Testament reminiscence, "Sir, I will assuredly be your disciple," but then he had disappeared. Another inquirer, a certain Fakeer who promised very well, never returned from a visit to his family. Perhaps he paid the price of his intention to be baptized. Europeans, Eurasians and Armenians had rejoiced his heart by declaring for Christ, and in Dinajpur he had been greatly cheered, as he was to continue to be for many years, by the declaration for Christ by Ignatius Fernandez of Portuguese descent. But until 1800 all Carey could say of the native population and of those who heard him preach in Bengali, was that "No one appeared to be awakened." He had been afraid, as many of his letters testify, that this lack of news of conversions might disturb the churches at home and affect the measure of support. But Calvinists were never among those who expected or demanded speedy results when the seed sown was the Gospel. Then the time of waiting ended and, so far as Serampore was concerned as the scene of Carey's labours, the waiting had not been long. The dreary time had been in Calcutta, Bandel, Soondarbans and Mudnabati. It was there that the ground was hard and the young shoots were quickly scorched. It was there that thorns sprang up and choked every promising growth. In Serampore, however, blessing came in less than a year, surely a confirmation of the move from Dinajpur. The seal was thus early placed on the new centre of mission operations. In the time of waiting, he found consolation in the parable of the leaven with its hidden processes slowly and silently maturing. He also used the parable in a letter to American Baptists in order to describe the work he was actually sent to do—namely, "to leaven the whole lump." How right he was in his application of the parable of the leaven to his work later years have showed. He may have made his sister feel when first he started preaching that he was another Gideon seeking to destroy the altars of Baal in a night, but, in India, he learned patience, the patience of the husbandman in the fields. This did not preclude direct preaching in the face of idolatry. At Malda, for example, in 1796 he addressed the gathering crowds from the steps of the temple itself and the folly and wickedness of idolatry was his theme.

He had to face the tragic and bitter problem of unbelief, particularly the refusal to believe on the part of those who had long waited for the Gospel to be proclaimed to them. It was this terrible problem of unbelief which, by its intractableness, had produced a theology of election for the few and damnation for the rest. It must be by the action of God Himself, so it was argued, that so many disbelieve. They cannot help it! It is God who denies faith to them. Carey, however, with a less rigid and fanatical Calvinistic theology, says during this period of stress and strain, as he finds his way to the deeper regions of faith, "When I first left England my hope of the conversion of the heathen was very strong, but among so many obstacles it would utterly die away, having nothing to cherish it but many things to obstruct it. unless upheld by God." One is reminded of Henry Martyn's letter, now in the library at Aligarh, in which he said, "I think I am willing to continue throwing the net at the Lord's command all the long night of life, though the end may be that I shall have caught nothing." Indeed, his faith never wavered as he rested all upon God. "Without His power," he insisted, "no European could possibly be converted and (He) can convert any Indian." He also defined his long-continued difficulties, and declared his living basic faith in the words, "I know that God can convert the obstinate and superstitious." In typical Carey fashion, he analysed the reasons why men found belief so hard, and the answers he gave himself were that the Brahmins feared to lose their advantages, the higher castes their prestige and the poor were in terror at the vengeance of neglected and abandoned debtas (spirits).

But in due course, as has been said, the break-through into Hinduism was successfully made. Krishna Pal, a carpenter, was baptized on confession of faith in the Lord Jesus Christ, at the age of thirty-five, in the Hoogli on 28th December 1800, along with Carey's son, Felix. The immediate agency of conversion was medical, for John Thomas treated successfully Krishna Pal's dislocated right arm while Carey assisted not only by prescribing medicines but by inviting Krishna Pal to visit the mission house that he might hear the Holy Bible expounded. Not only was Krishna Pal baptized, but also his wife, his wife's sister and four daughters, together with his friend Gokool, who had been won by Carey's preaching, and his wife and a widow who lived nearby, all caste Hindus. They were quickly in trouble for eating with Europeans; in fact, they were said because of this to have "become Europeans," but they persevered in their discipleship. The whole series of events comes to life in a letter from Krishna Pal himself and in an article in the Mission Journal written by Ward, while the nature of the saving experience itself is communicated by Krishna Pal's hymn. The sacred Ganges had been desecrated by the Christian baptism of a Hindu. Widows had found a different spiritual destiny from that of burning on their husband's funeral pyre. The missionaries rejoiced that "Thus the door of faith is open to the Hindus and who shall shut it? Thus is the chain of caste broken, and who shall mend it?" This first group of converts had many successors, including Petunder Singh, who not only became a preacher but an excellent schoolmaster also. Numbers of the lower castes also declared for Christ, and the first Muslim to confess Him, as has been said, was a certain Peroo. Then came a Brahmin, Krishna Prasad, who at the age of nineteen was baptized, breaking the seven-fold sacred cord and trampling it under his feet. He became the first ordained native preacher, and later he married Krishna Pal's daughter in the first inter-caste marriage. Other Brahmins also confessed Christ. By 1804 forty Indians had been baptized. Krishna Pal built the first native meeting-house in Bengal, and there were twenty others of his fellow-countrymen worshipping there beside the family. The names of the earliest church members who had all been baptized on "the credible confession of faith" and also of those described as "constant hearers" were printed in the second volume of the Periodical Accounts. How interesting and moving these lists are with their testimony to God's grace among the different castes, in family circles and with various types of personality. Then inevitably by the continuing movement of God's Spirit, churches came into being, gathered churches of converts. "It would give you great pleasure," said Carey to Fuller, "could you drop suddenly among us on an ordinance day and see the lively affections with which such a number of persons of different colours and nations unite in commemorating the dying love of Christ." Carey's doctrine of the church can be deduced from his correspondence with Harvey Lane, Leicester. The story of the pioneering effort in Calcutta that led eventually to the founding of the Bow Bazaar Church in Calcutta, shows Carey in characteristic action. It began in a bamboo shed in 1806 into which natives could freely enter and in which the preacher, very frequently Krishna Pal himself, used the vernacular. Crowds quickly gathered, and there were "a good many converts." As a result, however, of the Vellore Mutiny in 1806 and the massacre of British officers and men and the consequent fear of disturbances in other parts of India, preaching became forbidden in Calcutta and then later was confined to episcopally ordained clergymen. However, by 1809, the ban having been lifted after strong representations had been made from Serampore, the chapel was opened on the 1st January in that year. It was here that Adoniram Judson and his wife were baptized on 6th September 1812.

The letter dismissing Carey from Leicester to the newly formed church of Christ of five members "meeting at Mudnabati or elsewhere in Bengal" is a model of its kind. There was a revealing touch, however, in a sentence Carey wrote about the new little church, "We receive each newcomer with a kind of hesitating joy." There were storms, social as well as personal, material and economic as well as spiritual, before church members were "stablished, strengthened and settled" (1 Peter v. 10). There was at times bitter persecution. It was part of Sydney Smith's argument against Missions as conducted at Serampore that "a Hindu who becomes a convert to the Christian religion" is "subjected to present and worldly indignities; indeed, to the most perfect degradation," and he gave many examples. One would have thought that this witty and worldly cleric had never read either the Gospels with their injunction to take up the Cross or the Acts of the Apostles with their records of the sufferings of the earliest missionaries. But Serampore regarded what Sydney Smith presented as a disaster as a subject for doxology. But Sydney Smith rightly emphasized that "if conversion merely destroys the old religion without really and effectually teaching the new one," it is quite useless. With such a sentiment the Serampore trio would have immediately concurred and their practice with every convert disproved the wild charges he made against them. The converts also were themselves missionaries. Unlike the Church in the south of India associated with the legend of the Apostle Thomas, these new churches were at once concerned about the spiritual state of their neighbourhood and country. They were evangelical in theology and evangelistic in spirit. The missionaries might feel, as indeed they did, that the handful of converts was hopelessly outnumbered by the thousands and tens of thousands to be seen at any single Hindu Pujah. But they believed that it was only as Indians undertook the conversion of India that the great sub-continent could ever be won for Christ. "In my judgment," said Carey, "it is on native evangelists that the weight of the great work must ultimately rest." Later chapters in the acts of these nineteenth-century apostles, with names of people and places, with dates and events and with persecutions and blessings could be written recounting the ways in which these glorious hopes began to be fulfilled in Carey's day and of the ways in which in later years this same conviction regarding Indian evangelists is still firmly held.

II. The Translator

ON 5TH MARCH 1801, Carey laid reverently on the Communion Table in Serampore the very first printed and bound copy of the Bengali New Testament, "the first considerable book ever printed in Bengali prose." The labour of spelling, writing and printing, etc., in Bengali, quite a new thing and requiring decisions about orthography, had been splendidly overcome. Here was pioneering indeed. The aim, so much desired, which he had sought so long and which so frequently he had mentioned in his letters home, was at last fulfilled. The emotions of the Serampore trio as this was done went very deep and they made their joint achievement an offering to Almighty God. It was also their hope and belief that, with the New Testament in the vernacular, there might be more conversions, and indeed there were. Marshman spoke of the edition of two thousand as being two thousand missionaries.

Already, on the boat, Carey, who had none of the typical Englishman's shyness or obstinacy about learning languages, had been John Thomas's assiduous pupil in acquiring Bengali. He also declared his hope in a very early letter that his eldest son would learn Sanskrit, his second Persian and his third Chinese, and more than once he commented favourably on his sons' fluency in Bengali when very young. Over the six years in North Bengal, he had so prepared himself that by the time of his arrival in Serampore he had mastered Bengali not only as a spoken but as a written language also. Dialects were a bit troublesome. They bore, he said, "as much resemblance to the true Bengali as Lancashire to the true English!" It was typical of him that he sought first of all to give the New Testament to the people in their own ordinary tongue. He was of the same temper as his fellow-Englishman, William Tyndale, who said to a priest who challenged him, "If God spare my life, ere many years, I will cause the boy who driveth the plough to know more of the Scriptures than you do." But a true mastery of Bengali demanded a study of Sanskrit, "the great classical language of India and the main source of the great vernacular languages of Northern India." Carey was now beginning to enrich the language used in all Bengali homes, businesses and streets with closer derivations from the original Sanskrit. As a result of this more and more of the potentialities of Bengali which he described as "rich, beautiful and expressive" were realized. He began a Sanskrit Grammar and a Dictionary, and in a short time it could be truly said of him that he could speak Sanskrit as fluently as the Brahmins. It was part of his motive in learning Sanskrit that he might translate the writings accounted sacred by the Hindus, and in so doing show them to be "the mysterious, sacred nothings" (and worse) that they really were. It is of course true that a wider range of study has revealed a heritage richer than Carey knew. But Dr. A. C. Bouquet is surely quite mistaken in suggesting that Carey translated the *Ramayana*, of which it was said that "it brings those who sing and hear it to the highest state of happiness and finally to equality with the gods," out of respect for the myth and its chief character.

Thus in 1801 there was produced the first of the eight Bengali New Testaments issued during Carey's life-time. The work of translation that was to prove so prodigious had now begun. The reason why a Lectern could so fittingly be presented to and received by the Dean of Westminster Abbey in 1949 as a Memorial to William Carey, "Missionary in India and Translator of the Bible," had begun to have cogency. It had been Carey's practice as he acquired each new language, while still in England, to read his daily Scripture chapter in each of these tongues successively. His text book in learning these languages had been the Bible. The *Enquiry* was Biblically founded, and it was from the Bible, of course, that he took his text for the "Death-less Sermon." In fact his studies of language and his painstaking, patient effort to master them had as their motive a desire to publish the Word of God in speech and in print. Whatever else he translated was meant to sub-serve the Bible and to give it free course. It stood alone, Old Testament and New Testament together, and no other sacred book could be substituted as a prepara-tion for the Gospel. It was his source book, the food of his soul and the nourishment of the Church. From the earliest days he consciously realized that a convert of a Church without a Bible could never survive for any length of time; corruption of doctrine and practice, discipline and order, would quickly set in. Carey had predecessors in the translation of the Bible respectively for the people of India and of the adjacent island of Ceylon. And of course such inhabitants of India as the Portuguese had a Bible in their own tongue. Before his day the Bible had been translated into Tamil, the New Testament and the Psalms into Hindustani, and the New Testament and Pentateuch into Singhalese. There was also a manuscript of Matthew in Bengali from the pen of John Thomas. In the graphic words of S. Pearce Carey, this meant that before William Carey began his life work "only two lamps were burning" in the East. Carey and his colleagues, however, in the course of the years, built up a breath-taking and indeed unparalleled list of translations of the New Testament and of the whole Bible. In all, some forty translations into the principal languages and dialects of India and the East can be catalogued, and a history of each of them would yield an inspiring story. They followed each other quickly down the years, and Carey was the master-hand both in translation and in editing. He was the inspiration of the whole. He claimed that letter writing was only possible in time "stolen" from the translation of the Scriptures. To prove this he gave his correspondent the following time-table at Calcutta: "I rose this morning at a quarter before six, read a chapter in the Hebrew Bible, and spent the time till seven in private addresses to God, and then attended family prayer with the servants in Bengali. While tea was getting ready, I read a little in Persian with a moonshi who was waiting when I left my bedroom; and also before breakfast a portion of the Scripture in Hindustani. The moment breakfast was over, sat down to the translation of the Ramayana from Sanskrit, with a pundit, who was also waiting, and continued this translation till ten o'clock, at which hour I went to College and attended the duties there till between one and two o'clock. When I returned home, I examined a proof-sheet of the Bengali translation of Jeremiah, which took till dinner-time. I always, when down in Calcutta, dine at Mr. Rolt's, which is near. After dinner, translated, with the assistance of the chief pundit of the College, the greatest part of the

eighth chapter of Matthew into Sanskrit. This employed
me till six o'clock. After six, sat down with a Telinga
pundit to learn that language. At seven I began to collect
a few previous thoughts into the form of a sermon,
and preached at half-past seven. About forty persons
present, and among them one of the Puisne Judges of
the Sudder Dewany Adawlut. After sermon I got a subscription from him for five hundred rupees (£63 10s.)
towards erecting our new place of worship; he is an
exceedingly friendly man. Preaching was over and the
congregation gone by nine o'clock. I then sat down and
translated the eleventh of Ezekiel into Bengali, and this
lasted till near eleven; and now I sit down to write
to you."

He himself translated the whole Bible into Bengali,
the language of the most heavily populated province in
India; Oriya, the language of the most religious province of all, with its great Hindu centres at Puri, Kan-
arak and elsewhere; Hindi, the language of the great
northern cities; Marathi, the language of India's war-
riors and Sanskrit, the language of culture. The Chinese
translation was made by Joshua Marshman and completed in 1822. Carey never forgot that the Bible had
come to him as an Englishman in translation; the Old
Testament in Hebrew and the New Testament in
Greek. No wonder he took such steps in various capaci-
ties to give others the Bible in their own tongues. How
he delighted "to give a New Testament to men who had
never seen one before." Indeed, it was largely through
the inspiration of Carey's example that the British and
Foreign Bible Society was formed in 1804.

But it was not only the Bible that Carey translated
and printed. He needed text books for his Fort William
students, and some of these had to be from the Hindu

E

classics. Also, converts looked for helpful reading that would supplement the Bible and would be useful for distribution. To this end tracts and pamphlets, "all of them close addresses to the conscience," were published. These were carried about the country, Benares being particularly mentioned, by evangelists and missionaries. Some of these booklets presented the way of salvation, while others concentrated on "the errors of Hinduism and Mohammedanism." These evangelists were made in the same mould as Wycliff's poor priests sent out towards the end of the fourteenth century with the English Bible. The travels and experiences of these native evangelists in India as they carried the New Testament and other literature far and wide is yet another story that still remains to be told. Many of these Indian apostles suffered cruel persecution at the hands of their fellow-countrymen, hazarding their lives for the sake of the Name. (Acts 15. 26.) But they also had their moments of glory. In the neighbourhood of Dacca some of them found a handful of villagers who, though no missionary had ever been near them, had abandoned idolatry and indicated as the reason for this change in faith a little wooden box which turned out to contain a well-worn copy of Carey's first Bengali New Testament.

In February 1818 Carey consented, not without difficulty, to Joshua Marshman's publishing a monthly paper in Bengali which sought to provide reading matter for the increasingly literate general public. It had to be of a non-political kind, Carey insisted, and religious controversy must be avoided. Then, two months later, on the 31st May, the first newspaper (a weekly) ever printed in any Indian language, was issued from the Serampore Press. Lord Hastings declared the paper to be "extensively and importantly useful," and thus India got its first periodical, a publication that aided the development of the Bengali language and contributed to the moral and spiritual development of the people. Also, in April 1818, an English monthly magazine, the *Friend of India*, destined for a great future, was published.

In the very nature of the case, the earliest versions of the Scriptures needed frequent later revision, but such labour was congenial to the Serampore translators, since their language studies were always thorough and as complete as possible. Carey the Baptist, the one-time cobbler, would never have been appointed, without any competition at all, as the Professor of Bengali, Sanskrit and Marathi at Fort William College unless he had been competent for his duties in every way. Other members of staff had to be well qualified and so had he. None but a well-grounded and proficient linguist could have addressed in Sanskrit so eminent and brilliant an assembly as that gathered at the new Government House in September 1804. Nor could the students of William Carey have presented their effective "disputations" and "declamations" on this same occasion unless they had been well taught. Carey, by the way, held this post till 1831. Sydney Smith might jibe at "consecrated cobblers," but even he later had to acknowledge the solid and scholarly achievements of the Serampore trio. In any case his slanders were effectively answered by Robert Southey when he championed these "low-born and low-bred mechanics" who, in such a short time, had learned such a great variety of languages, and translated the Scriptures into so many Eastern tongues. They had done more in this field than "all the world's princes and potentates . . ." and "all the universities and establishments." Carey discovered and understood the principles on which languages were founded, and his grammars and dictionaries, as well as his translations, show him to have been the very opposite of the sketchy amateur. Described as "the creator of Bengali prose," he won personal fame by his Dictionary of the Bengali language. But there was also his Bengali Grammar and a whole list of works of a grammatical and lexicographical kind. On his arrival in Calcutta in 1793, one of his first acts had been to engage a pundit, and it was said of him in later days, "he wore out three pundits in a day." The well-known portrait of Carey by Home shows him with Mritunjaya, his chief pundit. Biographical sketches of these pundits of his would be of real value. In the *Enquiry* he almost dismissed as nothing at all the difficulties that others had advanced about foreign languages. It was not that there would be a gift of tongues, but as with traders so with missionaries old and new, there was no need of "extraordinary talents." Any language anywhere could be learned in a year or two, and in the interval there were such creatures as interpreters. His own practice can best be seen in his advice to his son Jabez . . . "Labour incessantly to become a perfect master of the Malay language. In order to this, associate with the natives, walk out with them, ask the name of everything you see and write it down; visit their houses, especially when any of them are sick. Every night arrange the words you get in alphabetical order. Try to talk as soon as you get a few words and be as much as possible one of them." Carey could never have been satisfied as was Kiernander the Swede in his twenty-eight years in Calcutta, brought as he was to that city by Robert Clive as "a missionary to the Portuguese," never to be able to converse in Bengali or Hindustani. As early as 1803, Carey, in writing to Ryland, declared that in about fifteen years it should be possible to have the Word of God translated in all the languages of India. In the actual event this time-table was left far behind.

This translation work of his brought inevitably certain other demands. A printing press and a printing staff were needed. Both type and paper required to be provided. Reference has already been made to the rough wooden printing press Carey had purchased for £40 while in Mudnabati and had brought with him to Serampore. This served the mission press for many years and it was on this press that the first Bengali New Testament was printed, both type and paper, however, being quite unsatisfactory. A skilled printer was available in the person of William Ward, who had come to India as the result of Carey's personal and prophetic invitation to him some years before. He remained till his death in 1823 in charge of the press. Brunsdon, by the way, had met his untimely death following a liver complaint caught from standing on an unmatted floor in the printing office. The story of the types that became available was quite a romantic story. A certain blacksmith, Panchanana, who had been taught by Sir Charles Wilkins, the distinguished oriental scholar, how to make excellent Bengali type, arrived at Serampore looking for work at the very moment when someone of his skill was needed most. With his aid a type foundry, for both old and new types, some of them very beautiful, was set up, and the mechanics of printing thus being to hand, material could be taken through all the necessary stages. Panchanana also proved a useful teacher of others, and Serampore, it was said, remained until 1860 "the principal type foundry of the East," most of the types being cast at Serampore for the very first time. As far as paper was concerned. Carey had begun by using "Patna" paper which, apart from being dingy, porous and rough, attracted book worm and white ants. In the attempt to manufacture paper themselves, the missionaries erected a treadmill worked by relays of forty men. Then a steam engine was ordered from England (Bolton, Lancashire), the first ever to reach India, and by 27th March 1820 it was in action. It produced what came to be called "Serampore" paper of good quality. Carey's personal life on the whole was free from accident and disaster, but in the evening of 11th March 1812, the buildings and presses, paper and books, founts of type, apparatus and much else, including many precious manuscripts, went up in flames. Carey was in Calcutta at the time, and on his return was told consolingly that a few punches and matrices were uninjured, but the labour of years had been consumed in an hour or two. The trio quickly rallied with characteristic courage and energy, and rapid steps were taken to effect recovery, Ward at once taking a long lease on a warehouse in the neighbourhood. At home, their cause was so splendidly and widely championed that in fifty days, and possibly for the only time in its history, the Committee had to cry, "Enough, enough." The fire really proved an advantage, for it gave the opportunity of retracing their steps so far as quite a number of projects were concerned. Also, as it were, in the glare of the tragic conflagration, the true nature of the activities of the Serampore brotherhood was dramatically and clearly revealed. This had some effect, it has been said, in securing the writing in of the freedom clause into the revised East India Company's Charter in 1813. As a consequence of the unrestricted opportunities now given them, the members of the Serampore team were able to continue for many more years their full missionary programme of preaching and teaching, itinerating and translating.

It is significant of the place that translation held in Carey's mind, interest and programme of work that in his letter to Steadman, under the date 1831, only three years before his death, Carey, giving reasons for not accepting his invitation to return to England, mentioned first of all his desire to see certain portions of the Bengali Bible through the press at Serampore and also his anxiety to see "completed at press" an edition of the Sanskrit Bible. Then, also, at an even later date, in the last year of his life, writing to his sisters in England, he said, "I am now able to sit and to lie on my couch and now and then to read a proof sheet of the Scriptures." By this time, in his closing months, he was preaching no longer, but the Word of God was still his daily joy and a labour of love.

III. The Educationalist

HOW NATURAL IT was that Carey the Bible translator should seek a reading public who could take individual advantage of the written word. He was appalled at India's illiteracy and he saw no future either for an illiterate Church or an illiterate nation. His own interest in books was life-long, and concern for education for himself and others was always near his heart. It was not surprising, therefore, that during his North Bengal period, he opened, and gave daily supervision to, the first primary school that India ever had. Previously there had been only a very few schools here and there at which, for example, a number of boys of the Brahmin caste had received brief religious instruction from their priests. Also a number of boys in trading circles had been taught to keep books. In Carey's school, tuition was free, Carey meeting the costs himself. The curriculum covered reading, writing and keeping accounts, and the scriptures were used as text books as well as for devotional purposes. Here was "the precursor of the Indian elementary school system subsequently established under Government auspices." What a sight it must have been to see the first shy yet eager group of bright-eyed youngsters assembling in makeshift premises with Carey, whose discipline had left so much to be desired at Moulton, taking charge, along with one or two native assistants. On this occasion, as on many others, he was a pioneer.

As in the fields of preaching, translation and strategy, so in the sphere of education, Carey's move to Serampore brought development on a wider scale. On 1st June 1800, a Free School, with teaching in the vernacular, was opened in Serampore under the care of Joshua Marshman (who had been a schoolmaster at a Ragged School) and his wife, both well qualified in every way. It soon numbered forty boys, mostly very young. Some of these were soon removed by anxious parents who feared that infant minds might be poisoned and that the children might be forcibly made Christians or even sent to England. Most fathers and mothers, however, were reassured on being told that the children would never be made to do anything that would make them lose caste. But what an anxious business it must have been day after day. A year or two later, however, the same school was able to report that it was being given liberal support by Europeans in India, who saw its value, and that there were three classes, the first consisting of children who had not lost caste, learning only the vernacular, Bengali; the second, learning to read and write English as well as Bengali; and the third, who were being instructed in Bengali as catachumens, with studies to follow in history, geography, astronomy, etc. Schools of this kind were encouraged on all mission stations based on Serampore, and it could soon be said that the Serampore missionaries were bombarded with requests for them. In a comparatively short space of time there were over two hundred pupils. The missionaries obviously did not underrate the importance of education for the work of the Kingdom. They felt it was a reasonable expectation that religious impressions received at school might very well be "the beginnings of salvation to the children themselves and to many

others." The schools, they believed, would feed the
Church and help to lay the foundation of a culture and
civilization far different from anything India had previously known. Some of the Brahmins continued to be
suspicious and to take alarm, but public sympathy
went against them and Carey claimed that there were
signs that a little leaven was beginning effectively to
leaven the lump.

Another line of development was boarding schools,
begun in 1800, first for boys and then for girls (not a
woman in India could read!), and here again the mission gave a lead. Children of mixed parentage, Anglo-
Indians, their parents in some cases having become
Christian, were especially welcomed, and the correct
pronunciation of English was to be given particular
attention! Fees, which proved a useful source of missionary revenue, varied from £45 to £50 a year,
according to the number of languages attempted,
namely, Latin, Greek, Hebrew, Persian or Sanskrit.
Here was indeed higher education at an advanced level.
Already in 1803, the first Sunday School for the teaching of catechisms had been begun by two of Carey's
sons, Felix and William, and the Portuguese, John Fernandez.

But to William Carey himself, a signal recognition
in the educational field came in 1801, when he was invited to become teacher (and then later, in 1806, Professor) of Bengali, Sanskrit and Marathi in the Fort
William College, which was to have a University curriculum of arts, sciences and law, and which had been
newly-created by the Governor-General, Lord Wellesley,
himself a product of Eton and Christchurch, Oxford.
The aim of the College was to rescue from dissipation,
profligacy and corruption, young Englishmen, civil and

military, who came to India at the tender age of sixteen to assist in its government and administration.
Lord Wellesley, who had arrived in India in 1798, desired that they should be trained (and trained in India)
in such a way that they would be equipped for the
tremendous responsibility they were to be called upon
to assume. In a three years' course, it was intended to
bring education, discipline, and principle into their
lives. It was a noble conception, and Carey's heart went
with it, but he could hardly believe his ears when it
was he, the one-time cobbler, the Baptist minister, the
missionary on sufferance, the non-academic, to whom
this high appointment, with all its opportunity, pay
and honour, was offered with the Governor-General's
approval. Nor could anyone have dared to prophesy at
that time that he would become the College's most
notable figure and its focal personality. The pay, £700
a year (later from August 1806 £1,500), he welcomed,
as did his colleagues, as money that might be devoted
to the Mission, and, during the years that followed, it
played a considerable part in financing the opening up
of new stations. When later he was given a stipend for
translating works from the Sanskrit, he devoted this
further amount to this same object. The opportunity
Fort William gave him he delighted in, because languages were his *forte* and teaching them would in-
crease his mastery for the purposes of translation. Day
by day he would share the company and tasks of
learned colleagues while outstanding pundits would be
assembled from all parts of India. In the event also, he
was the outstanding contributor to the one hundred
original volumes, grammars, dictionaries, reading books.
compilations and editions, including the Bibliotheca
Asiatica, which poured forth from Fort William. The

exalted character of the post he recognized would give him the chance of influencing India's future rulers and, indeed, a worthy list can be compiled of Fort William men, magistrates, judges, collectors of revenue and governors, who achieved distinction in India and elsewhere. It was not required of him that he should abandon his missionary purpose as a condition of appointment and, indeed, he tells Ryland in a letter that it was "as a missionary that I was appointed to the office". On the great occasion in 1804, in the presence of Hindu and Muslim dignatories in the marble hall of the Governor's Palace, he testified on the widest possible stage to his call and convictions. He held this appointment till 1830 when, on the College being reduced to an examining, and no longer a teaching, body, he was retired on pension.

Throughout the whole of his long Serampore period, his weeks were divided between Calcutta and Serampore. The week-ends he spent at Serampore busily engaged, along with Marshman and Ward, in Bible translation and preaching. Then from Monday evening to Friday evening he was in Calcutta where, in addition to his duties at Fort William, he preached whenever he could and often engaged in practical service in the prison and among the human wreckage of the streets. He travelled by boat between Serampore and Calcutta on the sacred river, weaving throughout the years a pattern of industry and discipleship rarely equalled. The rhythm of this alternation between these two centres, Calcutta and Serampore, gave him the opportunity of physical exercise, thus affecting his health for the better, while the regular change of scene, duties and companions was both refreshing and stimulating.

At Fort William he was employed professionally in

a college planned by others, but the time came when at Serampore he was principal for twenty-four years of a college planned, built and paid for by himself and his colleagues. On 15th July 1818 they issued a prospectus for "A College for the instruction of Asiatic Christian and other youth in Eastern Literature and European Science." Sanskrit and Arabic were to be taught in view of their basic relationship respectively to the literature of Hinduism and Islam, but the emphasis was laid on the vernacular. English language and literature were included, since it was through that language that a real entry into the world of scientific and Western ideas could be made. It was intended that manuals in scientific subjects would be produced at Serampore in the vernacular. Carey himself became Professor of Divinity and Lecturer on Botany and Zoology. The Serampore prospectus did not contemplate or anticipate the later view that "English might become the medium of Christian civilization in India." The College was a most daring innovation, representing perhaps, despite its many vicissitudes in later years, the most enduring memorial of the Serampore trio. Behind it was an educational policy that had been brought into operation at Serampore from the beginning of the Mission there. Actually it had already been adumbrated in Carey's earliest plans in Mudnabati. It was to be the apex of an educational system which had established a whole network of vernacular schools within a twenty-mile radius of Serampore, the pupils of which required, and requested through their parents in many cases, something more advanced. As a matter of fact the Serampore trio had been anticipated in this higher sphere of studies on its cultural side by the setting up in 1816 in Calcutta of a Hindu college by wealthy Indians who desired their children to be instructed in the English language and in European science. The West, with its wealth of new knowledge and its increasing technological skill, was beginning to appeal irresistibly. Lord Hastings, the Governor-General, who brought to his great task in India liberal views of education, not only was the inspiration of the movement that produced this Hindu College, but he gave his blessing to the Serampore project and agreed to become "first Patron of the College," with the Governor of the Danish settlement of Serampore as "first Governor of the College." Such a college had been seen by the missionaries to be necessary from the earliest days as "a consolidation of their plans." It was an instrument of mission required by their endeavours in preaching, translation and education, but there would be full religious liberty for all students and no constraints on conscience. That India and its millions could only be converted by its own people and not by a handful of foreigners was one of Carey's foundation principles, so both for the churches' sake and the schools', leaders and staff who were adequately trained were of paramount importance. The College would also possess a Library, and in the course of the years many treasures in both manuscripts and unique books have been accumulated. It would include a Teachers' Training Department, but it would have as its crown a Theological Institute with a four-year course for the training of Indian ministers and missionaries.

Through this agency, theological students would be thoroughly instructed, not only in their own beliefs, but in the beliefs that would oppose them. It was also felt to be highly desirable that future pastors should be trained in an institution where secular subjects were also adequately handled and not in a separated semin-

ary. Also they believed that it would be well for Arts
and Science students, whether Christian or non-Christian, to receive their education in a college where
Christian worship, Christian theology and Christian
principles were the inspiration of the whole. There was
a grandeur about this conception and it represented a
profound understanding of the meaning and the value
of university education. The charter given later
allowed for the right of development along independent
lines as a Christian university, a right accorded to no
other Christian college in India. Unfortunately, down
the years the whole conception of such a college with
its ideals and projects has often failed to find acceptance
in principle as it has had difficulty from time to time
in securing a sufficiently qualified staff. Dr Staughton,
for example, remitting money from America in 1831,
did so only on the limiting condition that it was not
to be spent on teaching science but on the theological
education of Hindu converts. Perhaps also the hopes of
its founders that non-Christians would be influenced by
Christian witness and character were set too high. Also
the College has never been sufficiently endowed. Nevertheless, its record has been noble and distinguished and
the Church in India and in other Eastern lands has
gained greatly from a ministry trained at Serampore.
It is, perhaps, true to say that at the time of writing
and particularly since China with its great Christian
universities, colleges and schools ceased to be a mission
field, the opportunities facing Serampore were never
greater, situated as it is so near the Burma border and
not inaccessible from other regions further East. The
building, so "adequate to its aims" and sited healthily
on the river side, was designed in Ionic style, and the
expenditure amounted to about £15,000, which was

covered by the contributions made by the Serampore trio themselves through private appeals or largely by their own earnings. The grievous controversy between the Home Committee and their missionary supporters on the one hand and the Serampore group on the other, which had already begun by 1818 and by 1827 had become a schism, prevented help for the running and maintenance of the college (about £1,200 a year) being mobilized in England on a grand scale. Only £3,000 or so was forthcoming. In fact, even when in 1837 the schism was healed and Serampore stations incorporated in the Mission, the College together with the actual station at Serampore was expressly excluded. But the great project went bravely forward with John Mack, a classical scholar from Edinburgh and a brilliant science teacher, serving from 1821 to 1845, first as tutor and then as principal, and with John Clark Marshman on the staff from 1819 to 1855. Government grants in aid of education on the secular side were obtained quite early. In America, some ten thousand dollars raised for Serampore were invested in American funds with American trustees. Denmark, also, on the personal representation of Joshua Marshman to the King in Copenhagen, granted a Royal Charter, embossed on vellum and richly bound, signed on 23rd February 1827 and read at Court in Fredericksnagore in June 1827, with the power to confer degrees. The power was not used for many years. Carey, in the year before his death, drew up a series of regulations for the College, thus ful-filling the King's requirement through the charter that statutes defining the powers of the College Council and settling the general principles of the management and government of the College be completed in ten years. In 1845, on the transfer by sale of Serampore to Britain

after some ninety years in Danish hands, the treaty safe-
guarded not only the rights and immunities of the College but its Christian character. In the first year, there
were thirty-seven students, nineteen Indian Christians,
fourteen Hindus and four said to be without caste or
religion. The all-India character of the College foundation sets it apart from other Indian colleges which are
territorial in range. Full advantage of this wise and far-
reaching provision of the charter has always been
taken. From the very first days among the students were
to be found Khasis, Garos and hill tribesmen. Also
young men from further afield than India have received
their education at Serampore, including students from
Ceylon and Burma. How significant also it was that the
first Indian principal was not a Baptist but a Syrian
Christian from South India. From the first it had been
agreed that there should be no denominational test for
professors and that, out of a council of five, one might
be non-Baptist. Carey's vision was never limited by race,
nation or denomination, and in the original Statutes of
the College are to be found the words, "No caste, colour
or country shall bar any man from admission to Serampore College."

IV. The Man of Conscience and Compassion

BEFORE HE LEFT England Carey had shown his sympathy for the African slaves by boycotting West Indian sugar, and he was never heard to pray during the whole of his life without heartfelt intercession for the victims of the sale and purchase of man by man. In the *Enquiry*, in a paragraph praising traders for their courage and persistence, the qualities needed in missionaries, he even points out that these characteristics are to be found in those who conduct "the accursed Slave-Trade on the coasts of Africa." There is far more evidence to show that he was moved to compassion by his reading of the New Testament than by study of Rousseau's *Social Contract* (1762) or Tom Paine's *Rights of Man* (1787), though doubtless he was familiar with both these books. From a distance also, he shared the movement in Britain and elsewhere for the abolition of the slave trade and for the freeing of the slaves in the Empire, rejoicing when Wilberforce and his friends won their Parliamentary victories in 1807 and 1833 respectively.

It was not surprising, therefore, that with a heart that could feel the sufferings of his fellow-men and women, an eye that could see their plight, feet that could never hurry past their need and hands ever ready to help, Carey was deeply shocked by the inhumanities which met his gaze and lacerated his heart from his very first arrival in India. He quickly discovered that widow-burning (Sati) and infanticide and other cruel practices were deeply woven into the pattern of Indian life and were indeed held in the general view to be expressions of Hindu faith. He was not unmindful, of course, that, in the England he had left, there were barbarities even in legal punishment that had been responsible for women being burned alive in the eighteenth century, either for witchcraft or the murder of their husbands. But the very first letter of Carey's, printed in the first Periodical Accounts, contains a reference to the horrors of Sati and other terrible customs. In the Spring of 1799, he actually saw in a village near Calcutta the immolation of a widow, in all its horror. He did everything he could by expostulation and appeal to prevent the tragedy being enacted, but the relatives, assuring him that the widow was acting voluntarily, replied in surly and increasingly ugly tones that he was witnessing an act of holiness. But it was indignation that he felt and not reverence. As with Abraham Lincoln and the sale of slaves, so in Carey, through the funeral pyres of widows, a determination was born that meant vigorous and finally successful action. He led a reform movement and, as was usual, he managed to win the support of others. Along with his Serampore colleagues, he sought to work on the public of England by detailed and harrowing descriptions of this all-too-frequent and so dreadful a practice. True to temperament, he carefully collected and collated reliable statistics on the basis of which it was estimated that, in Bengal alone, ten thousand women perished in this holocaust annually. Research in the Hindu classics established that this shocking custom was neither ancient nor obligatory. Armed with these findings, Carey and his friends made representations to

Lord Wellesley, the Governor-General, in his last few days of office, realizing that only Government could bring this practice to an end. The matter was submitted to the Judges of Appeal, and, in their report of 1805, they deprecated any action by Government that would interfere with "the religious opinions and prejudices of the natives." It is terrible to think that an interval of twenty-four years had to elapse before Carey was called upon in his official capacity to translate an Order in Council abolishing Sati throughout British Dominions in India. He received this document on Sunday morning, 5th December 1829, while he was preparing to take a service. One glance at its contents, however, showed him that even a few minutes gained in publishing the pronouncement would mean the saving of lives. Someone else therefore had to preach the sermon while he translated this long-awaited notice. Strong opposition inevitably developed among Hindus and the usual processes of appeal were strongly pressed, but in the end it was decreed that widows should no longer suffer this terrible fate. Custom, however, dies hard, and in 1955, when the writer was in India, the press carried a story of the police only just arriving in a village in time to prevent the law being broken and a new victim being immolated.

The cult of murder extended also to lepers, and there is a tragic and pitiful description by Carey himself, in 1812, of the burning of a wretched man in a pit with a fire at the bottom of it, the victim of his relatives' callous decision and cruel actions. Later on, in the spirit of the One who laid his hand upon a leper, Carey established a leper hospital in Calcutta, the first of the many for which the different missionary societies have been responsible.

It was at an earlier date that Carey, as the authority on Sanskrit, had succeeded, at the request of the Governor-General of the day, in establishing after careful research that the other terrible custom referred to above, namely infanticide, was not enjoined in the Hindu sacred books. On receiving this report, the Governor-General immediately declared such acts to be murder with death as the penalty. Thus it became illegal for baby girls to be starved, suffocated or strangled, or for infants to be exposed in the forest in baskets, or drowned, or thrown to the tender mercies of sharks and crocodiles. The drowning of the aged, whether by themselves or others, was also forbidden. One wonders what new thoughts were in the minds of the fifty Sepoys at the great Ganges Festival at Sagar as they successfully kept close watch to prevent the new law being broken by the huge crowd of pilgrims and worshippers.

At Serampore, as has been pointed out earlier, there was a Juggernaut shrine and, as at Puri, Orissa, there was the annual procession of the god and his spouse in a new wooden car driven by a frenzied team of devotees down the newly-swept road. There were many deaths annually as men and women, either in an ecstasy of self-dedication or drugged by others, flung themselves beneath the wheels to be maimed or killed. Here was a fearful side to idolatry. The pilgrimages also (and what would Hinduism be without its pilgrims!) were responsible for a yearly total of casualties, many of them fatal. Hunger, fatigue, illness and disease claimed their victims. Another evil to which Carey made early reference was what could only be described as "swinging on hooks." This was a terrible diversion practised by way of devotion and also entertainment at festivals and fairs. The acrobats had hooks passed through their backs and, bleeding and torn, and often drugged, they became human pendulums. It should be remembered, of course, that, in this same century in Carey's own England, there were such dreadful exhibitions as cock-fighting, bull-fighting and bear-baiting, and also public executions, death being the penalty for many small offences. Such terrible practices, whether at home or abroad, found in Carey an inveterate antagonist. While pressing always for legislation, he sought on deeper levels through the Gospel of Jesus Christ his Redeemer to win the men and women of India to a new evaluation of human life and personality, and to awaken in them conscience and compassion. To this end, he not only preached his Gospel, he also witnessed to it. He was a frequent visitor to the gaols. He set up benevolent institutions first for boys and then for girls. His whole system of primary education worked out with the skilled and experienced help of Joshua Marshman had something of the Robert Raikes' motive in it, since each of these men sought, the one by his Sunday schools in Britain and the other by his schools in India, to rescue waifs and strays. Carey, like Dr. Barnado later, had an ever open door and there were no barriers of race, colour, tongue or faith. His institutions soon began to return to society its rejects and outcasts, and in the years of its existence there were many who were re-habilitated and turned into useful citizens.

But there was another notable field, and field is the right word to use, where Carey made a distinctive and important contribution, namely in agriculture and kindred matters. It was obvious that he felt a slight touch of guilt about this side of his work, or at least apologetic, since he knew that "those whose souls were pant-

ing after the conversion of the heathen" would have
little sympathy with its more scientific aspects. He had
the heart of a countryman all his days, as his delight
at the sight of a daisy ("Bellis Perennis" as he so scien-
tifically called it), after thirty long years in India, clearly
manifested. He had shaken out over a patch of earth
in a shady place a bag which had contained various gifts
from an English gardener and, lo and behold, he found
a solitary daisy growing there. And so, during the years,
the boy of the Paulerspury collections of plants and
flowers became the highly-skilled and wonderfully well-
qualified creator of the Serampore gardens and the inspiration for many years of the Calcutta Botanic Gardens, where his bust in marble testifies to his outstanding services. He was in touch by correspondence with
the leading botanists of the world, seeking and giving
information, and he was familiar with their publica-
tions, some of which he edited. With many of them he
embarked on a series of reciprocal exchanges, he receiving such things as the seeds of nutmeg, coffee and
cloves and they yams, convolvulus, etc. In India itself,
he was always to the fore as a scientific botanist, as
could be seen from his "books of observation", from his
insistence on accurate names, his schemes of classifica-
tion and his experiments with crops (wheat, hemp and
jute) and with grafting, soils, manures, etc. Birds, also,
were one of his delights, as was the infinite variety of
insects. Flowers and shrubs, trees and plants arranged
according to the Linnaean system, were his recreation
as he traced and loved the work of God in nature. In
the evening of his days, when he could no longer walk,
his chair was carried into his garden for him to enjoy
its tranquility and beauty. As always, it remained for
him the place of prayer and meditation. How grievous

he found it, and how hard to bear, when his lovely garden, with all its varieties of flowers and shrubs, was flooded by three feet of water in 1823, and again in 1831, when it was overwhelmed, precious trees and all, in a cyclone. How ruefully he spoke of the probability of Brother Marshman letting cows into the garden when he himself would no longer be there to cherish it.

But this interest in the things of the soil was more than a hobby and more even than a scientific pursuit. It had its practical side, its human application and its reference to social and national welfare. He was all too well aware that India was a hungry land, even apart altogether from the periodic famines. It was also a land of much ill-health. Its inhabitants still number millions of folk who have never had a square meal in all their lives. Carey noted the scarcity of edible vegetables and of fruit, and in the course of the years, by skilful and knowledgeable cultivation, he worked miracles in size and quality. Not only had India a tyrannical land-system financed by money-lenders who, charging shocking rates of interest (as high as 72 per cent.), had families in their power for generations, but the method of agriculture was primitive. Carey even before coming to India had had no such childish illusions as Fountain, who had thought to sit in farmers' chimney corners, as he did in Rutlandshire, drinking milk! The culture and needs of the soil, the choice of good seed and the rotation of crops, the wretched farming utensils and the uncared for cattle, the whole matter of irrigation and of bringing waste areas under cultivation, and much more beside, cried aloud for Western knowledge to be shared. Carey set himself to give it in every way and proved himself a pioneer with many successors as he came to India's rescue.

He used his eyes, his Northamptonshire eyes, and saw the situation for what it was. He compiled scientific papers, sought publicity for them in learned journals, and was honoured by learned societies. Very soon he was writing home asking not only for seeds, cuttings and roots of flowers and plants of the English countryside, but also for the seeds and graftings of fruit trees, with detailed instructions how to pack them. Every new mission station in India and further afield became a new source of knowledge and supply. He was one of the first to advance schemes of afforestation, and his trees at Serampore were one of its glories. In his order sheet also, he included "instruments of husbandry," namely, "scythes, sickles, ploughwheels and such things." At the sight of India's starving multitudes in the cities and the under-nourished multitudes in the villages, Carey's conscience and compassion were deeply roused. He says in this same letter that all these things he was requesting would be "for the lasting advantage of what I now call my own country."

The story of his forming the Agri-horticultural Society in 1820 had much in common with his founding of the Baptist Missionary Society in 1792. Actually, as in the Enquiry, he quoted Brainerd and his assistance to his Indian converts in sowing their maize as his example. He had long had such a scheme in mind, but it was only when Lady Hastings played an Andrew Fuller part in respect of the enterprise that he felt able to go forward. At the meeting called in Calcutta to consider action in the matter, only seven, including Marshman and himself, attended (only half as many as in Widow Wallis's Parlour, Kettering), but with Carey as Secretary the project went forward. India's "abject and degraded" agriculture and horticulture, with the consequent near-starvation of her people, was henceforth challenged by a dedicated group, however small, whose knowledge was scientific, whose experience was detailed and practical, whose motive was compassionate and whose vision was compelling. But this group, the membership of which was open from the first to all races, realizing that only Indians could bring their country successfully through its agricultural problems, did all it could to teach and train the people of the soil as well as the landed gentry. Carey and his friends and colleagues were forerunners of the modern Western interest in "under-developed lands" and of the desire to share technological knowledge with the African and Asiatic. But both Carey's philanthropy and his concern for agriculture, however scientific, arose from his love for his Saviour.

V. *The Missionary Strategist*

IT WAS FULLER who said that the origins of the Baptist Missionary Society were to be "found in the workings of brother Carey's mind," and history adds that this creative and vigorous mind never stopped working to the end of his life. Not only could he plod, he could plan. If Napoleon in the same period was the military strategist who failed, Carey, with a vastly different empire in view, was the missionary strategist who succeeded. Though he had left England never to return, he continued to influence the situation there, not only in the Baptist Missionary Society, but also in his own and other denominations. In India, it was he who worked out the master plan of a chain of mission stations, who built up, with strong support from William Ward, relations with other Christians and finally who sought, as a necessary development of missionary organization, international and inter-denominational conferences every ten years.

What then happened in the Baptist denomination in Britain following Carey's departure with John Thomas in May 1793? Dr. Whitley, in his *British Baptists*, has said that from that event and all that belonged to it, "A wonderful change came over the denomination." The new spirit of evangelism made its presence felt on the home front also. One notable result was the formation, in 1797, of "The Baptist Society in London for the Encouragement and Support of Itinerant and Vil-

lage Preaching," later known as the Home Mission
Society. Its aim was to reach "the heathen" (precisely
so called) in the homeland. For them, the field was one,
as indeed it ought to be for every Christian, though different methods of approach and activity must be used.
Steadman and Saffery had already been commissioned
by Carey's foreign Missionary Society to undertake
tours in Cornwall, and they had been preaching in that
county, in private houses, streets and backyards, in
meeting-houses and town halls. An important development linked with 1792 and 1793 and the years that followed was the constituting of the Baptist Union in
1813, whose declared objectives included as a priority
the encouragement and support of the Missionary
Society. In the setting up of this first of all the Baptist
Unions, the leaders of the Baptist Missionary Society
took a considerable part, thus demonstrating further
their concern for the land of their birth.

The Society itself, under Fuller's brilliant and inde-
fatigable leadership, slowly made headway. Carey's
adumbration in the *Enquiry* of such a movement was
largely the pattern that was followed. London continued
to "drag its feet" and more than once Fuller sought out
some obscure back-street in the metropolis to hide his
sorrow when coldly received. It was hard work and the
writer, as Andrew Fuller's latest successor, is filled with
wonder at the courage and faith of this small, econ-
omically poor, socially insignificant and largely Midland
group, as they faced the task of building-up nation-wide
support. Was it wishful thinking that included on the
title page of the Periodical Accounts from the very first
issue, an advertisement that the publication might be
had of "the Baptist Ministers in most of the Principal
Towns in the Kingdom." Fuller found his burden some-

what lightened, however, when letters began to arrive from the field. After fourteen months' silence, material, interesting, picturesque and moving was to hand, and the first of the Periodical Accounts appeared in 1794, with its opening narrative of "the first establishment of the Society," its account of the Mission to Cornwall mentioned above, a collection of Hindu fables and, best of all, letters from Carey, Thomas and Fountain. In the light of later difficulties, it might have been better if more attention had been paid to the careful editing of letters from the field. Without this flow of vivid and searching items of news the work of Fuller and his fellow-committee members would have been a great deal more difficult.

Throughout Fuller's life-time (he died in May 1815), relationships between the holders of the ropes and the small contingent of their friends and brothers down the mine (Fuller's own metaphor) were ideal. No shadows fell across their fellowship in the Gospel until the advent of the Rev. John Dyer as the Society's Secretary. He served from 1817 to 1841. For some time it had been evident that a new attitude was beginning to manifest itself, but Dyer became its focus. His letters were described by Carey as "commercial" letters and the missionaries felt themselves to be ranked simply as "paid agents." The story of the totally unnecessary but entirely grievous controversy that broke out cannot be told here in any detail. It was perhaps inevitable that the ageing group of Serampore missionaries, with the splendid properties they had planned, built and paid for, the chain of mission stations under their control and their closely-knit community with its very special financial basis of arrangements, should have presented a difficult set of problems to a committee far away in

London, all the more so in that so few of the committee members now remained who knew the missionaries personally. It was a great pity that the suggestion
that Dyer should visit India was not followed up.
Younger men on the field, also, in the very nature of
the case, cannot have found it easy to reach satisfying
relationships with so closely-organized a group of older
colleagues who "dreaded the thought of a majority of
inexperienced persons" in their group. But there was
no excuse for their setting up in opposition in Calcutta itself, they might at least have sought the opportunities open to them so pressingly further afield.
All these matters could surely have been handled con-
structively, the Serampore trio being recognized as a
very special case. Henry Martyn's tribute to them is
very relevant here, not only in the honour he paid
them but also in the emphasis he placed on their singu-
larity and indeed on uniqueness. He said, "Three such
men as Carey, Marshman and Ward, so suited to one
another and their work are not to be found, I think, in
the whole world." But there was no statesmanship in
the Home Committee, and the characters of the three
pioneers were vilified, particularly Marshman's, and
Carey was invited surreptitiously by the egregious Dyer
to testify against his close colleague of so many years.
Carey's reply blended nobility with indignation. Dr.
Marshman went to England between 1826-1829 at his
own expense, but the committee treated him with in-
dignity as they had earlier treated Ward, when in England from 1818-1822, with coldness. Mrs. Marshman,
also, in 1820 failed to be received with due respect for
her work and with affection for her personality. John
Clark Marshman, her son, in 1822-1823 suffered the same
reserve. Questions of property and trusteeship, matters

of authority and control, were elevated above grateful recognition of the unparalleled services, sacrifices and, indeed, almost in any definition, the saintliness of these three men whose places in the history of India and the Church will ever remain secure. How sad and tragic it was that Ward first, and later on Carey and then Marshman, all died outside the fellowship of the Society that Carey had founded and which he and the other two had served so long. It was not until 1837 that the gulf between the Society at home and the Mission at Serampore was bridged, and then not fully.

But fortunately a happier note can be struck, for there were other happenings of great importance in Britain and elsewhere following 1792. Later dates can be listed recording the formation of other missionary societies, mostly of the same pattern as Carey's and with the same great object. It was not only a case of *post hoc* but, in a genuine sense, of *propter hoc*, for it was to Carey that either directly or indirectly they owed their inspiration. The (London) Missionary Society, formed in 1795 on an interdenominational basis, owed its origin to the publication in the first Periodical Accounts of Carey's first letter. North of the Border, missionary societies were formed first in Edinburgh and then in Glasgow. Robert Haldane was so moved as he read these same Periodical Accounts that he sold an estate with a view to missionary service. The Church of England was also caught up in this new movement and in 1799 the Church Missionary Society, as it was called later, was formed, its first Secretary being Carey's friend, Thomas Scott. Then followed the British and Foreign Bible Society in 1804 and the Religious Tract Society in the same year, societies which largely emerged from the same interdenominational groups.

Then, by 1818, the Methodist Missionary Society came into being, thus fulfilling in denominational terms the long-cherished hopes of Dr. Thomas Coke, whose inter-denominational project in 1784 of "a Society for the Establishment of Missions among the Heathens" antici-pated Carey's own schemes. It was not until 1816 that the General Baptists of the New Connexion followed the example of the Particular Baptists in the founda-tion of a missionary society which, after its first mis-sionaries had consulted Carey and his colleagues at Serampore, decided, on their recommendation, to start work in Orissa. Outside the British Isles also there were developments. In 1797 the Netherlands Missionary Society was "formed to assist the L.M.S.," and closely linked with it was the Society for the Propagation of the Gospel amongst the Jews. Then came developments in America mainly through Adoniram Judson; in 1810, in Congregationalist circles, and in 1814, after his bap-tism in Serampore, among the Baptists. Here indeed, on the world front, was a transformation scene, a scene that rejoiced Carey's heart away in India. Following 1792 and 1793, almost the whole Church suddenly re-recognized the authority of her Lord, received power from the Holy Spirit, identified regions overseas as spheres of responsibility and furnished resources in men and money. Nor has any of these societies listed above become a casualty during the intervening years.

On the field in far-off places, also, these denomina-tional missionary societies maintained close contacts in fellowship and service. In Moulton and Leicester, Carey had had a wide circle of non-Baptist friends and con-sultants, and how often when far away from them he named them all in his prayers. In India his friends in-cluded the distinguished Anglican, Henry Martyn, with his work among the Muslims, and the first official missionary of the Church of Scotland, Alexander Duff, so deservedly remembered in the cause of education. It was Ward who said, "I am more than ever anxious . . . to know no man after his sect . . . I would say of everyone who wears the image of Christ and who contributes to the improvement of the spiritual desert which surrounds him . . . the same is my brother . . ." They claimed that the shadow of bigotry never fell on Serampore. They felt it to be their "duty to forget the distinctions which divided society in England and to make common cause for the promotion of its (India's) welfare." Then they added, rather quaintly, "It will be time enough a hundred years hence when the country is filled with knowledge and truth has triumphed over error to think of sects and parties." When Bishop Heber, of Calcutta, lamenting "unhappy divisions" (perhaps the first use of this phrase!) and advancing the belief that reunion would bring before long "the harvest of the heathen" offered discussions on points of difference, Carey and Marshman replied accepting the invitation, though nothing came of it. It was Carey, however, who gave a lead, that, when finally taken up, has proved of immense benefit to the whole Church of God. The Missionary Society he had been instrumental in forming in 1792 could not, so he had felt, be other than denominational, nothing else being possible at the time in view of "private discords which might throw a damp upon their spirits." But already by 1805 he was proposing in a letter, the original of which may be seen in the vestry of the St. Mary's Baptist Church, Norwich, the holding of missionary conferences or "associations") every ten years of "all denominations of Christians from the four quarters of the world," com-

G

mencing at the Cape of Good Hope in "1810 or 1812 at furthest." He had seen the Cape of Good Hope from the ship *en route* to India in 1793. In support of this suggestion he declared that "it would be attended with very important affects and," he added, "we could understand one another better and more entirely enter into one another's views by two hours' conversation than by two or three years' epistolary correspondence." For once he failed to carry Fuller with him, Fuller declaring that though he admired Carey's proposal "as a pleasing dream," he could not approve of it. In such a conference he declared, "There would be no unity without which we had better stay at home." However, the future lay with Carey's idea, though not as emanating from him, as the Edinburgh International Missionary Conference of 1910, a hundred years later, and the formation of the World Council of Churches in 1948 have proved.

It was in the conception of a series of radiating mission stations, however, that Carey, as early as 1803, gave further decisive proof of his brilliant strategy. By the time of his death, these stations actually numbered eighteen. Serampore was the base of operations. There was never any thought of it being a closed circle, nor, on the other hand, was energy to be diffused over impossibly wide areas. Within a radius of one thousand miles, sub-stations were to be planted two hundred miles apart, each resident missionary and his Indian colleagues (in later years trained at Serampore College) operating within a range of one hundred miles, and each sub-station was to contemplate further extension. Control and direction were to be exercised from Serampore (this was one of the difficulties of the younger missionaries), and regular reports of both "spirituals and temporals" were to be furnished. The sub-stations were to be financed by the labours of the missionaries on the pattern of Serampore itself. The revision of the East India Company's Charter in the British Parliament in 1813, a successful battle in which Wilberforce in the House of Commons, Lord Wellesley in the House of Lords and Fuller with his petitions and propaganda played conspicuous parts, gave the Serampore missionaries freedom of movement at last and removed the insecurity that had haunted their efforts. The result of this was that Carey's plan already in process of development, as at Agra in 1811, could now be openly pursued. A detailed survey of this inspiring and adventurous campaign, with names, dates and events, so far removed from "missionary vagrancy," is long overdue. In a measurable time, there were three great chains of mission stations. Bengal had stations at Serampore, Calcutta and Monghyr, etc., together with Dinajpur, Dacca and Chittagong (now of course in East Pakistan) and Assam. There was also a chain of stations along the sacred Ganges in Hindu and Buddhist strongholds, among them Gaya, the scene of Buddha's awakening, Patna, where Sarasvati, the goddess of learning, is still especially honoured, Benares, the city of the Golden Temple and a multitude of other shrines, Allahabad, the confluence of the Ganges and the Jumna, and Delhi itself with hopes also of Lahore and Kashmir and their Muslim populations. Each of these cities had its array of temples, its army of priests and holy-men, its sacred places and its pilgrims. Orissa, as has been said, had been left to the General Baptists, and Agra was surrendered, in happy agreement, to the Church Missionary Society. It was always Carey's belief that the key to India's conversion lay in evangelism by Indians, but he saw clearly the need for foreign help. With his whole missionary strategy in view, he constantly pleaded in letters home for reinforcements, male and female (what an innovation in the early nineteenth century).

This same generalship was revealed by Carey in his aim of evangelism on a world scale. In the *Enquiry*, it was the whole world, whose statistics he tabulated, as it was the entire globe he pictured on his maps at Moulton. As early as 1794, on receiving appointment at the Malda indigo factory, he wrote home suggesting that now that his salary would be set free for other purposes rather than for himself, other mission work in "Sumatra or some of the Indian islands might be possible." In 1800 he wrote, "I have not mentioned Sumatra, Java, the Moluccas, the Philippines or Japan, but all these centres must be supplied with missionaries. This is a very imperfect sketch of the wants of Asia only, without including the Mohammedan countries, but Africa and South America call as loudly for help." Here was his world mind in operation. He never forgot the Tahiti or the West Africa that had first drawn him as the scene of his labours. China he sought to serve by translations, and Marshman's activities in this field were outstanding.

The Judsons, after being baptized at Calcutta, went to Burma, preceded by others including Carey's own son, Felix, who later in Carey's phrase, "shrivelled to an ambassador." Another son, Jabez, laboured in Amboyna from 1814 to 1818. William Robinson, after service in Bhutan, went to Java in 1813 and in 1821 left for Sumatra. To this island also there sailed in 1818, Nathaniel Ward, William Ward's nephew, with printing apparatus. He was joined later by Richard Burton of London and Charles Evans of Bristol. All these missionaries in the East Indies, and the Serampore trio also, had the sympathy of Sir Stamford Raffles, founder of Singapore.

VI. The Man

CAREY WAS A dedicated man. He may have used an eighteenth-century vocabulary to describe his call to follow Christ, and his spiritual pilgrimage may have had much in common with his contemporaries, but, in any age and setting, his consecration would have shown forth clearly. "Let God employ me," he said, "where He thinks fit and give me patience and discretion to fill my station." The Christian minister, he believed, must go where God pleases. His call to serve his fellow men in the widest definition and range came to him in his conversion. Like the Apostle Paul, there was no need for him to struggle with himself; his battle was first with those of his own family and denomination, then with the East India Company, and always with the general spirit of the age. Unlike the Apostle Peter, who never became anything more than a reluctant and hesitating missionary to the Gentiles, Carey from the start thought in terms of world mission. Having put his hand to the plough he never looked back, persuading many others in the different denominations to share his task. He worked, as someone has said, like a law of nature. He was the final opposite of a Dryden's Achitophel who "was everything by starts and nothing long." Like his contemporary, Robespierre, he was unswerving and incorruptible, but he was never cold, inhuman or remote. There was a spiritual logic that worked itself out stage by stage through his early preaching, his *Enquiry*, his "Deathless" Sermon, his decisive part in the formation of the Baptist Missionary Society and in his being the first volunteer from the denomination at home in the first months of the new Society's existence. Captain Cook's life was a record of voyages into places and situations and then quickly out of them again, but Carey stayed the course localized in India. As a Fort William Professor, for example, he never asked a rest or a holiday. Nor did he ever come home on furlough. If it could be truly said of Fuller that "He was a martyr to the Mission," it could be said with equal truth of William Carey. To it he gave, without stint and without faltering, forty-one years of continuous and unflagging service. He counted the cost and he paid it to the end.

But this same sense of Divine call, guidance and support made him humble-minded. "If God used *me*," he said, "no one need despair." After many years in India, someone in government circles asking the snobbish question, "Let me see, Mr. Carey, were you not once a shoe-maker?" received the modest but crushing reply, "No, sir, only a cobbler." He found difficulty when it came to the matter of a portrait of himself, and the brief inscription in the Serampore cemetery was by his own express directions. He could see no reason why his name should be remembered or perpetuated. He was "best forgotten," he said. He objected as firmly as he could when his friend, Dr. Roxburgh, named a tree after him, "Careya Saulea." His remarks at the end of his life to young Mr. Duff at once revealed the secret of his inner faith and the quality of his humility. He said, "Mr. Duff, you have been speaking about Dr. Carey, Dr. Carey. When I am gone say nothing about Dr. Carey —speak about Dr. Carey's Saviour." For his refusal to

print anything of a specifically religious or devotional
kind he gave as his reason his fear lest his life or character might suddenly belie the things he had dared to
write. He even went so far as to say in the manner of
the Apostle Paul (1 Cor. 9. 27) that he often feared
that instead of being instrumental in the conversion of
the heathen he might sometime dishonour the cause to
which he had given himself. Related to this profound
humility was his view of himself as a pioneer. He was a
David assembling materials for a succeeding generation.
Others would follow him and it was for him to blaze
the trail even if, as he said, the paths were rough. His
grammars, dictionaries and translations were tools for
later generations, his schemes of teaching and training
would help to prepare a body of Indian Ministers and
Missionaries whose work would largely lie in the years
he himself would not be there to share. His strategy in
devising a chain of mission stations was a provision of
the mechanics of mission, the development of which
would be in the future. The churches he helped to
gather were of the twos and threes and perhaps the
thirties and forties, but the larger companies would be
seen by his successors.

His life, however he himself might have regarded it,
was a signal record of solid achievement. He may have
written himself off as not among "those who are strong
and do exploits," but history makes its own assessment
in very different terms. There is something that seems
almost ludicrous in his confession to Ryland that indo-
lence was his prevailing sin, and in his insistence to
Fuller that he had "something of a lethargic disease." If
this were indeed the case, then day after day for a life-
time he won a conspicuous victory over his besetting
weakness. His young sister had said of him that, as a

child, he finished everything he began, and this plodding and persevering temper of his never left him. Mr. Old, at Hackleton, kept on view in his shop as a model of good workmanship a pair of shoes that Carey had made. Of the *Enquiry*, it might be said that Carey fulfilled it in life, character and service. He was the type of visionary who implemented his dreams. India's trying and debilitating climate was met with daily calmness and daily time-table. Carey's achievements in all the departments of his missionary service, in the College and the Press, the line of mission stations, the imposing list of translations, the social reforms he strove for, the botanical gardens he so greatly loved and the educational establishments he founded always demonstrated how honest, painstaking and thorough was his work. Though he cannot be said to have led others into new theological thinking as Fuller did, or to have launched new educational theories or method like Lancaster, in the realm of action he excelled.

His biographers are faced with a succession of carefully drawn plans and purposes, a series of dates and an array of facts of a precise and definite kind. That he can so properly be described as the most versatile of all missionaries is a well-deserved tribute to the interesting variety of his activities, co-ordinated as they were in his fully-integrated personality and his determinative goal. It was in reply to surprise that someone expressed at his command of so many languages that he declared, "Few people know what may be done till they try, and persevere in what they undertake."

But how did he stand up to adversity? He was not called upon, like the Judsons and many others in the long story of missions, to face imprisonment and torture. The threats of the East India Company, even if fulfilled, would not have resulted in any of the dreadful items in the Apostle Paul's list of his sufferings at the hands of his persecutors (2 Cor. 11.). Southey made this point in his defence of Serampore in the Quarterly Review, though he added that if martyrdom had come, there would have been no shrinking from it. Carey was never called upon to testify to his faith before cruel tyrants. But he had to face for long years the hardship and strain of "foes of his own household." Not only was his first wife never at one with him in his obedience to the overseas call, but for most of her time in India she had to be kept under restraint. This was also the sad fate that befell John Thomas. Then the leaders of the Society at home and his younger colleagues on the India field literally cast him out, along with his Serampore colleagues. In the whole of this controversy, however, Carey showed a calm Christian front. He was able to make a sacrifice of his feelings as well as of everything else. It was an early declaration of his that if his conduct would not vindicate itself, it was not worth vindicating. He never employed the weapons that were used against him by his antagonists. He was always seeking reconciliation. He starved in Calcutta; he had fevers in Mudnabati and in Serampore; he was the victim of at least one serious accident; he saw his lovely and precious garden twice engulfed by floods; he had to face the loss of manuscripts and types in the Serampore fire; he stood by helplessly while his savings and investments were lost in the Calcutta business crashes, and all too frequently he had to bear the death of a well-loved colleague and to comfort the bereaved. But in all these things he was "more than conqueror"; not, indeed, in the histrionic fashion of a W. E. Henley thanking God for his unconquerable soul, but as it were, noiselessly and without self-advertisement. Nothing ever finally broke him or even reduced him, even though he might cry in agonized tones, "The whole dead weight lies on me." It must be remembered, also, that to such a sensitive soul as his there was agony in the very fact of heathenism, and in its obstinate and dreadful realism, though it threw him back on the Word of God. He felt its pressure almost physically; it was something that could almost be breathed in. Its age-long character in Hinduism, Buddhism and in Islam, and its hold on social life and the family, and on the work of the fields and the factories, all revealed its tremendous and organized strength, but William Carey remained hopeful and unafraid with his faith unimpaired. It was the service of God in which he was engaged, and the issue was always in Divine hands.

There were many testimonies during his life-time to Carey. There was the recognition of his worth by a number of Governors-General in India, and particularly by Lord Wellesley who, by his own declaration, esteemed tribute from Carey a greater honour than the applause of Courts and Parliaments. There were the tributes paid to him in the House of Commons by Wilberforce and his friends in 1813 (though others vilified him). "I do not know," said Wilberforce, "a finer instance of the moral sublime than that a poor cobbler working in his stall should conceive the idea of converting the Hindus to Christianity, yet such was Dr. Carey." There were also the robust phrases of the poet Southey in his reply to the sneers of Sydney Smith, the renowned wit of the day. Again, there was the curious fact that in the long-drawn-out controversy between the Home Committee and the missionaries at Serampore, Dyer, the Secretary at home, never attacked Carey directly;

he was unassailable. A testimony by a non-Christian Indian might well be added at this point. He described Carey as "a rare spirit crossing barriers of national prejudices." But perhaps Carey can be seen most clearly mirrored in the qualities he himself declared to be those most needed in a missionary. In the *Enquiry* it was required he said that:

"The missionaries must be men of great piety, prudence, courage and forbearance; of undoubted orthodoxy in their sentiments, and must enter with all their hearts into the spirit of their mission; they must be willing to leave all the comforts of life behind them, and to encounter all the hardships of a torrid, or a frigid climate, an uncomfortable manner of living, and every other inconvenience that can attend this undertaking . . . and when arrived at the place of their destination . . . by all lawful means to endeavour to cultivate a friendship with them, and as soon as possible let them know the errand for which they were sent. . . . They must be very careful not to resent injuries which may be offered to them, nor to think highly of themselves, so as to despise the poor heathens, and by those means lay a foundation for their resentment, or rejection of the gospel. They must take every opportunity of doing them good, and labouring, and travelling, night and day, they must instruct, exhort, and rebuke, with all long suffering, and anxious desire for them, and, above all, must be instant in prayer for the effusion of the Holy Spirit upon the people of their charge . . ."

In a very early letter home, he emphasized that a missionary must be one of the companions and equals of the people to whom he is sent. Then also in a letter to his son Jabez in 1814, as he commenced work in Amboyna, Carey, with a father's intimacy and an apostle's discernment and experience, made abundantly clear the whole duty of a missionary at all times. His long career in India stands up in spirit and in detail to close investigation in the light of the demands he felt to be necessary and vital in the life and character of every missionary. When he died on Monday, 9th June 1834, surrounded by his friends, Indian as well as European, and full of years, he declared that all his desires were satisfied. Perhaps in his own modest way he was repeating the Apostle Paul's great words (2 Timothy iv. 7): "I have fought a good fight, I have finished my course, I have kept the faith."

But what of the spirit of the man? "this cheerful little man," as Lady Hastings described him at the very end of his life. The clue to all he was and all he did was the secret place. He always emerged from the unseen. He had first made contact with his Maker before he faced his daily relationships and duties. Everything he did had its inner side. His habit of constant and detailed introspection which belonged to his century may have resulted in everything being "sicklied o'er with the pale cast of thought," but there was nothing unhealthy about his spirit nor wanting in his resolution in every enterprise "of great pith and moment." He may have said of himself "I have enough in myself to discourage me for ever," but he never gave up. He may have advised his son Jabez to "pay the utmost attention at all times to the state of your mind," and also to obtain "a deep sense of your depravity," but his counsel was as full of robust common sense as his life was of decisive action. Prayer was his "native breath," but he was not of a mystical temperament, although in England he shared fellowship for a time with some followers of

William Law, with whose own emphasis on intention and act he had the fullest sympathy. Both in the opening sentence of his *Enquiry* and in the first of its concluding practical paragraphs, he refers to prayer. He had shared the response to the Prayer Call in 1784 issued by the Association and he traced its influence thankfully in many directions. In the *Enquiry*, he declared that the most glorious works of grace had always come in answer to prayer. He regularly held prayer meetings in his study, and when Alexander Duff visited him he requested prayer, as was his usual practice. Like the Apostle Paul, he often asked for prayer for his colleagues and himself, and he insists in one of his letters that he and his colleagues be prayed for "as a body." Church worship and fellowship also meant a great deal to him, and the lack of "social religion," as he called it, in the earlier years in India, left him much the poorer week by week.

But always, whether alone or in the congregation, in his garden or at church, it was his Redeemer and Saviour with whom he had communion. His theology was Christological; his message was the Cross and his fellowship was with the Risen Lord. It was the Atonement that gave him his gospel; it was to fulfil Christ's command that he formed a Missionary Society, and it was at His call that he went himself. His consuming aim was to win men and women of every race and colour, tongue and faith to the One who had died for them, their only Saviour, and to help them to enter the eternal kingdom of His love. So as Carey would have wished, this story ends not with himself but with his Saviour.

INDEX